A PRACTICAL GUIDE TO AIRLINE CUSTOMER SERVICE

A PRACTICAL GUIDE TO AIRLINE CUSTOMER SERVICE

From Airline Operations
to Passenger Services

Colin C. Law

Stamford International University

Hua Hin Campus

BrownWalker Press

Irvine • Boca Raton

A Practical Guide to Airline Customer Service:
From Airline Operations to Passenger Services

BrownWalker Press/Universal Publishers, Inc.
Irvine • Boca Raton
USA • 2018
www.brownwalkerpress.com

978-1-62734-693-1 (pbk.)
978-1-62734-694-8 (ebk.)

Edited by Doris Wai

Cover design by Ivan Popov

Typeset by Medlar Publishing Solutions Pvt Ltd, India

Publisher's Cataloging-in-Publication Data
provided by Five Rainbows Cataloging Services

Name: Law, Colin C.
Title: A practical guide to airline customer service: from airline operations to passenger
    services/Colin C. Law.
Description: Irvine, CA: BrownWalker, 2018. | Includes bibliographical references.
Identifiers: LCCN 2017958088 | ISBN 978-1-62734-693-1 (pbk.)
    | ISBN 978-1-62734-694-8 (ebook)
Subjects: LCSH: Airlines--Customer services. | Airlines--Management.
    | Consumer satisfaction. | BISAC: BUSINESS & ECONOMICS/Customer Relations.
    | BUSINESS & ECONOMICS/Industries/Hospitality, Travel & Tourism.
Classification: LCC HE9780 .L39 2018 (print) | LCC HE9780 (ebook) | DDC 387.7--dc23.

Table of Contents

Preface

A   *Practical Guide to Airline Customer Service* is written for airline executives, university lecturers and undergraduate students who are preparing for jobs in the service industry related to airline operations. Professionals who are currently working at airports or hotels can benefit from this book through understanding the importance of customer services within the airline and the service industry. This book primarily focuses on the customer service aspects of airline services. These include basic operations, essential communication skills, and how airline staff should interact with passengers at every contact point of their travel process.

This book provides an insight to the theory of customer service skills and communication skills, as well as customer service techniques utilized at three main customer touchpoints: the reservation center, at the airport and in the aircraft cabin.

A Practical Guide to Airline Customer Service is designed to complement airline companies' existing training programs. The key functions of this book are: 1) create students' interest in a career in this field, 2) provide the critical technical knowledge to prepare students for quick assimilation of specific carrier and customer service skills, and 3) develop the essential mindset one needs in order to excel in this field of service.

The first four chapters of the book outline the theory of communication, background knowledge of customer service and customer care, the airline policy of consumer protection and customer behavior.

The first chapter discusses the importance of customer service in the airline industry and explains the changes in the industry of transportation industry and its effect on the customer service industry. Chapter 2 of the book looks into the theory of communication. Chapters 3 and 4 explain the theory and the guidelines of customer care as well as some techniques that service agents can use to interact with customers. Chapter 5 details consumer protection policies that regulate the airline industry, whilst chapter 6 explores the different types of customers and their unique characteristics.

The second section of the book focuses on the service techniques at different touchpoints where airline service staff interact with customers.

Chapter 7 looks into the working environment in a customer contact center. Chapter 8 describes the airport working environment and the various customer service touchpoints within an airport terminal building. Chapter 9 explains cabin crew's responsibilities at different phases of a flight.

The last section of the book is divided into three different chapters, with the purpose of allowing readers to have a better understanding on how to handle customer complaints and methods used by management teams to evaluate existing customer service strategies, as well as contemporary customer services.

Chapter 10 provides advice on different approaches of handling customer complaints, dealing with angry customers and anger management issues. Chapter 11 looks into the various means of collecting feedback from the customers so as to improve service standards. The last chapter focuses on frontline employees' selling techniques as well as changes in expectations of customer service within the industry.

A Practical Guide to Airline Customer Service seeks to encourage students to pursue an exciting career in the airline industry. It is also a tribute to all the diligent frontline employees in the airline industry.

About the Author

Colin C. Law is an Assistant Professor of Airline Business Management at Stamford International University, Thailand. Prior to joining the academia field, he had worked in the customer service, reservation and finance departments of a major international carrier for nearly ten years. This extensive experience in customer service and airline operations has enabled him to develop multiple airline courses for the tertiary education sector and provided working professionals with insight into the airline industry. Colin is also the author of other critically acclaimed textbooks on airline airport operations, and is the co-author of *Introduction to Airline Ground Service*.

Acknowledgments

I would like to express my gratitude to the following individuals who have in their own ways, provided support and assistance and in helping to make *A Practical Guide to Airline Customer Service* possible.

I would like to thank Doris Wai for helping me in editing and proofreading matters. Thanks to Jeffrey Young, my publisher who encouraged me to pursue this book project.

Many thanks to Grace, Tony, Eva and Wylie for sharing their invaluable personal experiences, of which have formed the basis for the numerous case studies and the dialogues featured in this book.

Last and not least, I would like to thank all the air travelers who I have crossed paths with during my time working at the airport. Thank you for providing the inspiration for *A Practical Guide to Airline Customer Service*.

Introduction

Chapter Outline

Learning Objectives

After reading this chapter, the reader should be able to:

- Understand the nature of airline businesses
- Recognize airline customers' hierarchy of needs
- Understand customers' expectations
- Identify tangible and intangible customer services
- Identify an airline's internal and external customers

AIRLINE AND ITS NATURE OF BUSINESS

During the development of the aviation industry in the early 20th century, an airline was a transportation company that offered transportation service to the customers by air. Air transport was not common at that time as people were afraid of flying due to the many accidents that had occurred. The general public still preferred to take trains and ships for long-distance travel. The main goal of an airline in the early years was to carry customers from one place to another place safely. With the low market demand, the majority of airlines at that time were either established by the government or partially funded by the government. According to the report of Airbus Commercial Aviation Accident 1958–2015, the number of accidents decreased steadily over time.[1] As the industry became mature with improved technology, air travel has also become the safest mode of travel.

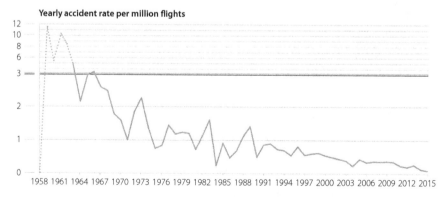

Figure 1-1: Airbus—A Statistical Analysis of Commercial Aviation Accidents 1958–2015 (Source: Airbus).

Today, air travel is one of the most important transportation systems in the world.

An airline is similar to an ordinary business in the service industry; the majority of the profits are from customers. After the deregulation of the airline industry in the 1970s, governments minimized their control of state-owned airlines and allowed private companies to establish their own new airlines. As such, airlines are free to enter the industry and intense competitions are created.

Customers' demand and expectations of airlines have vastly changed today. In the early stages, safe operation was the main expectation of the customers. As many airlines have improved their safety records, customers began to expect more from an airline company. Today, other than basic safety needs, customers are also demanding for comfort and top-notch services.

The Maslow's hierarchy of needs has defined that an individual's needs are segregated into multiple levels. We are motivated to achieve certain needs and that some take precedence over others. Our most basic need is the first thing that motivates our behavior and once that is fulfilled, it is our natural instinct to seek to move up the hierarchy and satisfy the other higher needs. Based on the same principle, an airline's hierarchy can be used to demonstrate customers' expectation of an airline.

Figure 1-2a: Airline's hierarchy of needs.

AIRLINE CUSTOMERS' HIERARCHY OF NEEDS

Airline offering safe transportation services is the minimum expectation of customers. This is also identified as the basic needs of customers in air transportation.

When the safety needs are met, customers' demands are then expanded to facilities at the airport and on-board the aircraft. Customers evaluate the airline by the types of hassle-free facilities available at the airport as well as the in-flight entertainment system, seat sizes and selection of meals served.

This is then followed by personal service or customer service. The way that customers are being served has a direct influence on customers' satisfaction level toward an airline. This includes the satisfaction with the interaction between customers and service agents, and service agents' problem resolution abilities.

Once the personal service need is fulfilled and customers are satisfied with the airlines' service, their intention for return repurchase is motivated and customer loyalty is established.

The very top of the hierarchy extends to long-term desires. Customers establish a long-term relationship with airlines when they are unlikely to change suppliers. In this instance, they feel important as they have become a VIP for the airline. This also reflects the customer's status within the airline company. The privilege status creates a stronger motivation for customers to return to the same company for their future travels.

Fulfilling customers' personal needs are not sufficient today as airlines are looking toward generating and retaining loyal customers. Loyal customers help airlines to secure and create a stable income for the company. The larger base of loyal customers generated by an airline, the better revenue it is likely to achieve. Many airlines today are putting a lot of efforts on satisfying customers' personal need and to motivate them to move up to the 'loyalty' and 'status' portion of the hierarchy.

APPLYING THE MODEL

To achieve customers' satisfaction, it is essential to understand their expectations. An airline company is offering services to thousands of customers every day and customer has different expectations when in face with different situations, and their needs are not always the same.

Safety
Customers fleeing from an earthquake disaster or situations pertaining to armed conflicts expect an airline to offer a safe transportation to

take them away from the affected areas. These customers have low expectations as their main travel purpose is to get to safety. Safety needs are the principal concerns and other needs are not as important to these customers.

Facilities
Customers travelling with their families on vacations will evaluate the type of services offered by the airline before making a decision. This is to ensure a comfortable ride. More often than not, these customers expect food to be served on their flights, some form of entertainment to be provided during the flight to keep passengers entertained, and someone to assist them during their entire journey.

Personal service
Customers who have been traveling with the same airline several times expect service agents at the airport to remember them by name and know their seating preferences. In this case, the standard of service offered by the service agent needs to be the same, if not better as compared to their previous travel experiences.

Loyalty
This applies to customers who fly so often that they decide to fly with the same airline whenever they need to travel. They make their decision largely based on their satisfaction with an airline and the services that the service agents offer. Even though there are other airlines operating similar service with a lower ticket price, customers are still willing to pay more using services from the same airline as they are very satisfied with what they are getting. They also offer recommendations to their friends for the excellent service offered by the airlines.

Status
These customers have gained a high status in the airline. They have flown so often that service agents at the airport and on the aircraft remember their travel details. All the service agents know their travel preferences and have them prepared in advance. These preferences include the following observations: Customer A always arrives at the airport for check-in

1 hour and 10 minutes before the flight; she has no check-in baggage; she always chooses seat 11A by the window and that she always has a Krug Champagne during her meal and a black coffee after that.

WHAT ARE CUSTOMERS EXPECTING?

Air travel is becoming more common today and customers have many choices of airlines to choose from. However, the aircraft manufacturing and cabin interior industries are dominated by a few players and airlines have no alternative but to offer standardized products in these areas. As such, they compete against each other by offering similar products in terms of cabin ambience, meal service, seat design, in-flight entertainment and communication technology. To generate competitive advantages, today's airlines are focusing on customer services to influence customers' choice of airline.

To win the hearts of the customers, airlines have used different strategies to keep their existing customers and attract new ones. The main objective is to ensure that the customers are happy so that they will return for repurchase and use their service again.

Customers' expectations

Satisfaction is generated after a customer enjoys their journey and feels the money paid is worth the value. The minimum customer expectation of an airline is supported by three basic elements: safety, timeliness and price.

Safety is the number one priority for all airlines. This demonstrates the trustworthy of the airline's operations, including aircraft

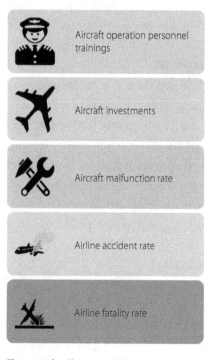

Figure 1-2b: Elements of airline safety.

(Figure content)
- Aircraft operation personnel trainings
- Aircraft investments
- Aircraft malfunction rate
- Airline accident rate
- Airline fatality rate

maintenance and security procedures. Customer will choose airlines, with the best safety records. These records can be easily accessed by customers via the Internet. Other details customers look out for include personnel trainings, aircraft investments, aircraft malfunction rate, airline accident rate and the airline fatality rate.

There are many modes of transportation for customers to choose from and the main reason for deciding to travel by air is usually time-related, i.e. customers expect to reach their destinations in the minimal time needed. Customers expect their flights to depart and arrive on time. As such, an airline's on-time performance data is an important factor when customers decide on their choice of airline.

Cost is another important element that determines customers' satisfaction. This is especially so for those who travel for leisure as this category of customers are price sensitive and customers seek other alternatives when an airline charges a higher price. Many airlines today have applied the yield management approach to target different customers by offering different pricing schemes to suit the needs of different travelers. Hence, customers who are taking the same flight and on the same service class may not be paying the same price for their tickets. These differences in prices are due to dissimilar ticket conditions. A customer paying a higher price gets more flexibility for their travel. These include enjoying the flexibility of date change, flight change and refund. On the other hand, customers who purchase discounted tickets are bounded by travel restrictions such as the lack of flexibility in terms of flight changes and refund.

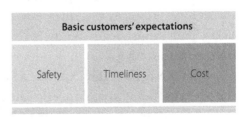

Figure 1-3: Basic customers' expectations.

Furthermore, today's customers have higher expectations. Other than the basic requirements mentioned above, they have additional demands such as service, quality, action and appreciation.

Customers constantly compare the airline service with the amount of money they have paid for their tickets. Generally, customers who have paid more demand a higher service needs compare to those who pay less.

Customers also compare service providers and choose the company with a positive reputation in terms of service and product quality. The quality of an airline is determined by variety of activities and offers offered, which are used as a basis for customers to evaluate the airline company as a whole.

In addition, customers expect airlines to take prompt actions when a situation arises and that they are be able to contact airline staff easily to have their problems resolved.

Customers wanted their business to be appreciated. These appreciations often create and strengthen the relationship between the airline and the customers, leading to future businesses. This is vital in an industry where an airline's quality and reputation can be easily spread by word of mouth.

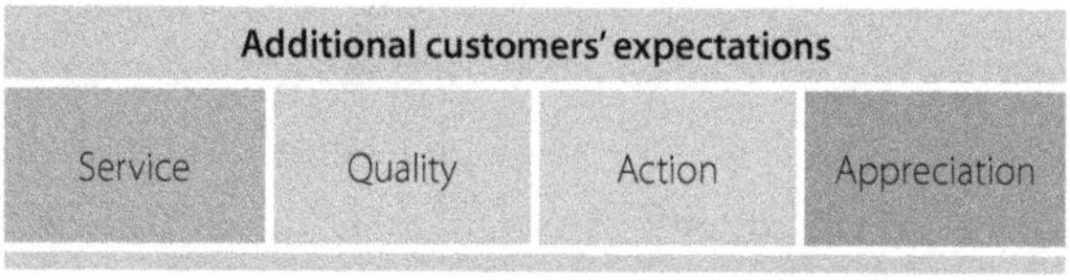

Additional customers' expectations			
Service	Quality	Action	Appreciation

Figure 1-4: Additional customers' expectations.

Each customer creates their own expectations of an airline's service. The minimum expectations that all customers have are concerns pertaining to safety and on-time departure and arrival. However, the level of expectations may not always be the same for all customers as this is a variable that is directly affected by how much they have paid for their flight ticket. Their satisfaction is directly influenced by whether the money they have spent is worth it.

Naomi Karten, a highly experienced speaker and seminar leader, has suggested the below formula to calculate customers' level of satisfaction.[2]

$$Customers'\ Satisfaction = \frac{Airline's\ Performance}{Customers'\ Expectations}$$

If customers' level of satisfaction is one, the airline is fulfilling customers' expectation. When the customers' satisfaction is more than one, it means that airlines' performance is exceeding the customers' expectation, and vice versa.

For example, on a flight from Asia to Europe, a customer who has paid several thousand US dollars on a ticket often has much higher expectations than another who has spent several hundred US dollars. As such, airlines offer different level of services such as first class, business class and economy class to fulfill their expectations. Airlines also arrange for special check-in counters for customers who have paid a higher fare and amenities such as lounge access and welcome drinks while boarding are offered to ensure these customers' comforts are met. Once an airline's performance exceeds customers' expectations, satisfaction is created. However, if the same airline fails to deliver as expected, the feeling of dissatisfaction is generated.

Flight from Singapore to London

Expectation	Airline performance	Airline performance
Customer A—Premium fare		
Flight departs on time at 0900	The flight departed at 0856	Flight departs at 0940
10 minutes wait to check in	6 minutes wait to check in	15 minutes wait to check in
Board ahead of another customers	Priority boarding offered	15 minutes wait for boarding
Disembark first	Disembark first	10 minutes wait to disembark
10 minutes wait to retrieve baggage	8 minutes wait for baggage	20 minutes wait for baggage
	Exceeds expectations = Satisfaction 👍	Did not meet expectations = Dissatisfaction 👎
Customer B—Low fare		
Flight departs on time at 0900	The flight departed at 0856	Flight departs at 0940
30 minutes wait to check in	16 minutes wait to check in	45 minutes wait to check in
30 minutes wait to retrieve baggage	28 minutes wait for baggage	35 minutes wait for baggage
	Exceeds expectations = Satisfaction 👍	Did not meet expectations = Dissatisfaction 👎

Customers' in-flight expectations are generally set by the industry. Today's customers' basic expectations of an airline are safety, comfortable chairs, delicious food, in-flight entertainment, and enthusiastic service agents. However, the industry's expectations are changing rapidly. When one airline introduces a new product, other airlines follow quickly. This then becomes the new industry standard. To draw an example, when one airline offers in-flight Wi-Fi service and in-seat power ports, the airline booking soars. Other airlines soon start to follow and these eventually become the basic services provided in an aircraft. Customers' expectations are also influenced by the type of services purchased. The cost of air tickets differs vastly among first-class cabin, business-class cabin, economy class cabin; and between full-service airlines and low-cost carriers.

Standardized cabin amenities

First class is the most luxurious class that seeks to provide customers the most space and comfort on an aircraft. This premium service comes with a price and the cost of first-class tickets is usually the most expensive. Due to the cost of the ticket, customers who travel by first class have very high expectations in terms of the airline's products and services.

Business class is the second-tier class and majority of the customers are frequent travelers who go on business trips. These customers also set high expectations as they are familiar with the airline's operations and know what to expect from airline service agents.

Economy class is the most inexpensive class and is attractive to a variety of customer types, including families, tour groups and on occasions, people who are travelling for business purposes. Traveling by economy class is not as expensive as other classes and the majority of customers have lower expectations. Occasionally, there are businesspersons and other frequent travelers who choose to travel by economy class and these customers often maintain their high expectations as opposed to other economy-class customers.

Full-service airlines are airline companies that offer a full packaged service to customers. After customers purchase their tickets, a majority of other services such as in-flight meals and allowance for check-in luggage are offered free of charge.

On the other hand, low-cost carriers offer limited service and only cover the basic product. If a customer needs additional products or services, they are required to pay an extra fee.

In short, a customer who has paid to travel on a full-service airline has higher expectations than another who decides to fly with a low-cost airline as the former is also seeking comfort and amenities on board the aircraft. Low-cost airline travelers are aware that the amount of money they paid only covers the transportation process and these customers required to buy other amenities for more comfort if they desire.

WHAT IS CUSTOMER SERVICE?

Customer service is defined as a series of interactions between a product provider and its customer at different stages of a sales transaction. The American economist, Robert W. Lucas has defined customer service as the ability of knowledgeable, capable and enthusiastic employees to deliver products and services to internal and external customers.[3] To ensure that transactions are performed smoothly and efficiently, employees who are involved in said transactions must be talented and keen to perform their duties.

Figure 1-5: Customer service cycle.

Customer service is becoming significantly important in creating customer satisfaction in many airlines today. In this context, customer service refers to the process of service delivery to customers before, during and after the purchase of an air ticket. Customers often use this experience to determine an airline's quality of service and decide whether they will purchase tickets from the same company for their future trips.

Customer service is an integral part of the profit cycle, helping an airline to achieve its goals. When customers are satisfied with the service provided by an airline, this will guarantee a subsequent purchase. This in turn, increases the airline's revenue and it can then use these profits to offer incentives to employees and further motivate them to keep up their good work, improve the airline's image by carrying out marketing campaign and social responsibility programs, and improve their products. The continuous cycle not only retains long-term customers, it also helps to maintain the airline's profitability and encourage growth.

In the airline industry, a customer's level of satisfaction is based on a combination of tangible and intangible services.

Overall, customers are expected to spend less money and arrive at their destination on time and safely. Many airlines have achieved all the three basic elements effectively. When these elemental elements are met, customers then raise the bar and demand more from the airlines. To fulfill customers' additional demands, many airlines are offering supplemental benefits. These additional benefits can be divided into two categories: tangible and intangible products.

Tangible products are physical objects that can be perceived by touch and the five senses, i.e. something that customers can see, hear, smell and touch. This normally refers to the environment the customer is experiencing while using the airline's service.

Figure 1-6: Tangible and intangible customer service.

Sometimes the actual product they receive when using the airline service is accounted as a tangible customer service. Examples include quality of in-flight meal, availability of leg space in the cabin and the quality of the screen provided for in-flight entertainment.

Intangible products are products that cannot be touched, and they are often referred to as services. Services provided by airline service agents are also known as customer service. These include how customers are being served and treated throughout their journey. Examples include the efficiency of ground service agents performing the check-in and the helpfulness of cabin crew who offer in-flight services. Another influencing element is delivery of products and services, such as attitude and the helpfulness of airline service agents, and their ability to resolve minor issues and conflicts.

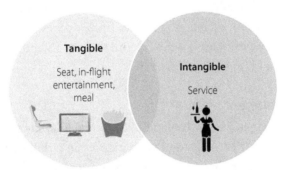

Figure 1-7: Tangible and intangible products.

Tangible products can be easily matched by competing airlines. Standardized seat pitch and width, hi-tech in-flight entertainment system and delicious meals are becoming the norm within the industry. These lead to airlines competing against one another on the basis of intangible customer services.

How a product is being delivered is as important as the quality of the product. Customers judge the quality of a company mainly based on the service that they get. This is especially so in instances which customers is flying with an airline for the first time. They will often evaluate the quality provided based on the service offered by the sales agent. For example, a customer would like to visit Sydney and has never been there before. This is also the first time he is flying and has no knowledge about making reservations for his first flight. He contacted several airlines' reservation departments to inquire about his trip. As the airlines are offering similar products at the same prices, he will eventually decide to fly with the airline which the reservation agent offers the best customer service as that is his best point of reference. The excellent service provided by the sales agent has resulted in his confidence in the airline, hence causing him to make the final decision to fly with a particular airline.

Tangible customer service
Product quality

The overall product that a customer purchases is evaluated based on its quality. A product's quality consists of multiple elements that motivate customers to purchase a particular service from airlines. These elements include an airline's reputation, safety record and the amenities offered both on the ground and on board an aircraft.

Service environment

This is also known as the service landscape or ambience. It refers to the physical locations where a customer experiences an airline's products. These may include the check-in counter's setup, airport lounge's layout, boarding gate's design and aircraft cabin interior's design, just to name a few. The environment also plays a part in influencing customers' overall perception of the airline and the chances of retaining return businesses. According to a psychological study of human behavior affected by the environment conducted by Albert Mehrabian in 1974, a customer may react in one of either two directions when making a decision: approach and avoidance.[4]

Approach reactions are generated when customers are satisfied—they are happy with the environment, e.g. state-of-the-art cabin facilities and appealing interior design of the aircraft, and are willing to stay longer or return for future occasions. On the other hand, avoidance reactions are created when customers do not enjoy the surroundings, e.g. crowded and dirty airline lounge. Below are other examples of approach-avoidance factors that customers consider:

- **The layout and design of the check-in area at the airport has a direct impact on customers' level of satisfaction.**
  The design of the common and individual queue areas have a direct impact on customers' waiting time.
- **Airline lounge service is only available to high-yield customers.**
  The design and the facilities in the lounge will affect customers' level of comfort while waiting for boarding. Customers who spend their time in the lounge prefer a spacious and private environment for rest or to work.
- **The boarding process used by the airlines impacts customers' level of satisfaction.**
  The boarding procedures adopted by airlines include boarding by rows, by zone or by random. Using different strategies has both positive impact and negative impact on passengers' waiting time at the boarding gate.
- **The color theme of the aircraft cabin and the background music is instrumental in creating a memorable travel experience for customers.**
  A clean and modern-looking aircraft also helps in raising customers' level of satisfaction.

Cabin Identify of Thai Airways International
In 2014, Thai Airways rebranded their aircraft and incorporated elements of the Thai culture in their new business class and economy class cabins. Thai teak wood, silk foil, rattan and Thai artwork were used in the cabins to reflect Thai culture and traditions so as to create a strong motif and brand identity.[5]

Figure 1-8: Airline's service environment.

The service environment is also dependent on employees' moods and the quality of the service they provide is often affected by the conditions of the working environment. Therefore, a clean, safe and well-designed environment can have an indirect impact on customers' level of satisfaction and impression of an airline.

According to Mary Bitner (1992), the service environment consists of multiple factors that affect customers' satisfaction. These include ambience, use of spatial space, functional congruence, signs and attires.[6]

Ambience

The ambience refers to the physical environment conditions. This includes all elements related to temperature, humidity, air quality, smells, sounds and light that influence customers' perceptions. While the ambience at the airport's check-in lobby is controlled by the airport authority, the airport lounge environment and the cabin environment can be adjusted based on individual airlines' preferences and needs. The cabin's temperature, pressure and humidity and lighting are also adjusted according to the time of the day to make the customers feel more comfortable.

Space

All customers prefer to have more privacy and space. The layout design of the check-in lobby, furnishing arrangement in the airline lounge and aircraft cabin setup also affect customers' level of satisfaction. A waiting area that is spacious and well-designed conveys a sense of openness and vice versa for one that is cramped and littered. An aircraft with too many seats may be unattractive to the customers as even though the airlines may be earning additional profit from the sale of these seats, the amount of space offered to the customers is compromised.

Functional congruence

Functional congruence refers to how well something with a functional purpose fits into the environment in which it serves that purpose. In the instance of an airline, this includes the functioning of the equipment used, the locations where check-in service is provided, availably of check-in kiosks at the airport and the distance from the airline lounge to the boarding gate. These come together to form the entire service experience.

Signs

Clear display signs are extremely important in an airport. While these are already put in place by airports, some airlines do provide their own signs to further assist and direct passengers to the correct boarding gate. In the aircraft, signs are installed to inform passengers when to fasten their seat belts and when they are permitted to use their electronics during the flight.

Attire

As ambassadors and representatives of the airline, it is essential for employees to be well-dressed and well-groomed. Some airlines also implement dress codes for passengers who are accessing the airline lounge as well as boarding of an aircraft. For example, Qantas has enforced the smart casual dress code for customers who wish to access the lounge.[7] American Airlines forbids customers who are dressed inappropriately or barefooted from boarding the aircraft.[8]

> Airlines set strict dress code policy for staff who travel on their aircraft. Staff who travel on the company's travel benefits are considered the representatives of the airline and they are required to dress appropriately. In March 2017, an airline was slammed in social media for refusing two female staff passengers wearing leggings to board the aircraft. They were asked to change their outfit before they were allowed on-board.

Service delivery system

An airline must deploy adequate service personnel to reduce waiting time. For example, the average check-in time for Airline A is 3 minutes. If it allocates 10 check-in counters to check in 500 customers, the total time required is 150 minutes. On the other hand, if it decides to open up 5 more check-in counters, the total required time is reduced to 100 minutes. However, the downside to this is increased airline operating cost. Similarity the number of cabin crew deployed on an aircraft affects customers' level of satisfaction. Another factor that determines services is the quality of the actual service delivered.

Intangible customer service

Intangible customer service mostly refers to the ability of service agents.

Service skills

Service skills refer to the ways employees interact with customers. These include communication skills, ability to maximise resources and think out of the box, and problem-solving skills. Today's customers expect service agents to understand their needs and resolve issues in a timely manner.

Product knowledge

In order to provide excellent service, airline employees must have adequate product knowledge related to their duties and the surrounding environment so as to cater to the needs of passengers. These include basic knowledge such as operation of in-flight entertainment system and duty-free limit allowance of alcoholic drinks allowed to be taken into a country.

Service attitudes

Helpfulness and friendliness are the basic requirements of a service provider. A positive mindset also helps to create a cheerful environment which indirectly helps to enhance customers' level of satisfaction. Service attitudes can sometime turn an unpleasant situation into an opportunity for creating loyal customers.

WHO ARE THE CUSTOMERS?

Customers are individuals or organizations who have engaged an airline's services. An airline customer can be from any group, gender, nationality or culture. In addition, airline customers can be divided into three types: internal customer, intermediate customer and external customer. It is important to establish relationships with both internal and external customers as the former handles all the various aspects that come together to create a smooth flight experience, and the latter provides the revenue that keeps an airline operating.

Internal customers

Internal customers comprise the following groups of people that airline employees work with in order to operate smoothly: vendors, suppliers, and manufacturers. In the instance of frontline service agents, they need the support of their internal customers—various supporting service agents to provide effective customer services to customers. These supporting service agents include catering service agents, maintenance personnel, baggage handlers and ramp agents. The airline also relies heavily on these suppliers who provide services for cleaning and catering to maintain the cleanliness of the aircraft and timeliness delivery of in-flight meals.

Intermediate customers

Passengers sometimes transfer between airlines, especially for long-distance travels and airlines need to work together to ensure a hassle-free experience. Hence, airlines need to consider the needs of their intermediate customers—other airlines. Teamwork is important in the airline industry as service agents need to coordinate with their co-workers to provide services to passengers.

Travel agencies and freight forwarders are also an airline's intermediate customers as these companies help the airline to sell its product to external customers. As such, it is vital to develop a good relationship with the providers of these services. This is even more so in today's context where customers' choice of airlines are directly influenced by travel agents and freight forwarders' recommendations. Offering excellent services and being attentive to these intermediate customers helps build good working relationships and increase sales.

External customers

These refer to the millions of customers who travel by air every day. While these customers expect to be well taken care of during their journey, there are some customers who require more help than others. It is important for airline service agents to identify these different types of customers, their characteristics and needs.

External customers may be divided into the following main categories:

- Business travelers
- Leisure travelers
- Cargo customers

Business travelers

These are customers who travel for work. These customers often travel many times in a year and are very familiar with the air travel process.

Characteristics:

- Dressed in formal attire
- Expect a hassle-free experience

Leisure travelers

These customers usually travel for leisure and in groups. They do not travel often and may sometimes require additional assistance.

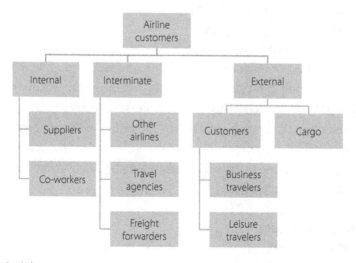

Figure 1-9: Airline customers.

Characteristics:

- Dressed casually
- Expect a fun and exciting experience

Cargo customers

Cargo customers engage an airline for freight delivery services and usually contact the airline directly. They are just as important as business and leisure customers as they make up a significant percentage of an airline's sales.

CUSTOMER SERVICE IN THE AIRLINE INDUSTRY

During the air travel process, airline employees from various departments have direct and indirect interactions with customers. The air travel process begins with customers making their ticket reservations. This is followed by check-ins at the airport, boarding of aircrafts, the en-route experience, arrival at their destinations and finally, baggage retrieval. There are airline employees at every step of the way who provide services and assistance to customers in distinct ways.

For example, reservation service agents must have superb listening skills as they need to pay attention to customers' requests. Both airport service agents and cabin crews require a different skill set as they deal with customers face-to-face. On the other hand, lost and found agents need to demonstrate strong problem resolution skills as the majority of customers who they are in contact with have issues with their baggage.

Passengers
Customer care (reservation and ticketing)

The customer care department, also known as 'reservation unit' is where customers contact an airline to purchase flight tickets. Traditionally, flight reservations are made by phone and reservation service agents assist customers to reserve their seats. Today, the majority of air tickets are sold through the Internet. However, when customers need to make changes to their travel plans, the quickest way is to contact the airline reservation centre directly. Hence, the reservation department also serves as a hotline which customers can contact the airline directly when they have any queries.

Customer care includes the following functions:

- Make reservations
- Ticketing arrangements
- Frequent flier points redemption
- Inquiry hotline

At the airport

Many airlines have reservation service agents stationed at the airport to assist customers with reservation and ticketing inquiries. They also take care of ad-hoc requests such as rebooking of flights.

Airport reservation and ticketing includes the following functions:

- Make reservations
- Ticketing arrangements
- Frequent flier points redemption

Check-in counter

On the day of departure, customers go to the check-in counters of the respective airlines to check in for their flights. Airline ground service agents then check their travel documents before issuing them a boarding pass. Customers can also choose to deposit their travel baggage at the check-in counter.

Check-in service includes the following functions:

- Registering customers for the flights
- Travel document checks
- Issuance of boarding pass
- Baggage check-in

Boarding gate

After going through the airport security and immigration (on international flight only), customers will then proceed to the boarding gate and wait to embark on the aircraft. During the boarding process, airline ground agents will need to verify customers' travel documents. They may sometimes collect a portion of their boarding pass for cross-checking of passenger headcounts.

Boarding service includes the following functions:

- Assist customers on embarking the aircraft
- Travel document checks

In-flight

While en-route a flight, cabin crews are stationed to ensure the safety and comfort of customers. The cabin crew demonstrates the usage of emergency equipment and offer amenities to customers during the flight.

In-flight service includes the following functions:

- Ensure safety of passengers
- Offer in-flight amenities and ensure customers are comfortable during the flight

Arrival

Upon arrival, customers will disembark the aircraft and airline ground agents are available to offer assistance to both arrival and transiting customers.

Arrival service includes the following functions:

- Assist customers upon disembarkation
- Offer directions to all customers

Baggage retrieval

After clearing immigration, customers can then retrieve their baggage from the baggage hall. Lost and found agents are stationed in the baggage hall to offer assistance to those whose baggage either did not arrive or were damaged during the flight.

Baggage service includes the following functions:

- Track delayed or lost baggage
- Make arrangements for return baggage
- Make arrangements for baggage repair

After-sales

Customers may sometimes contact airlines to feedback on their positive and/or negative experiences during their journey. For some airlines, agents stationed at the reservation departments are in charge of taking in these comments and resolve complaints.

Figure 1-10: Travel process for travelers.

Cargo

Customer care

While the process of cargo movement is similar to that of passengers, there is very limited interaction between the airline service agent and the cargo companies. Most of the communication and coordinating works are carried out over the telephone.

Reservations

Freight forwarders usually contact airlines for reservation. The sales team will then calculate the delivery cost and make the necessary arrangements.

Cargo reservation includes the following functions:

- Cargo space reservation
- Inquiry hotline

At the airport

Departure

Cargo is accepted at the airport's cargo terminal. After the documents are checked, the cargo will be stored in the terminal. They will then be loaded onto the respective aircrafts.

Cargo departure service includes the following functions:

- Cargo acceptance
- Inquiry

Arrival

Upon arrival at the destination, the cargo will be offloaded from the aircraft and stored in the cargo terminal. Freight forwarders will then need to submit their documents for verification before the freight is released.

Cargo arrival service includes the following functions:

- Cargo release
- Inquiry

After-sales

Freight forwarders may sometimes contact an airline to inquire about the status of their goods. These enquiries are taken care of by the after-sales department.

Figure 1-11: Travel process for cargo.

THE IMPORTANCE OF CUSTOMER SERVICE IN THE AIRLINE BUSINESS

According to statistics released by travel fare aggregator website, Flight Scanner,[9] a total of 228 flights carry passengers from Bangkok to Hong Kong every week and 12 airlines offer direct service between the two cities. The majority of these airlines offer similar facilities on their flight and are competing against each other on the basis on the cost of flight tickets and the quality of the services provided.

This shows that service is a critical factor that allows customers to distinguish the differences between airlines operating on the same route. If customers are satisfied with the service provided by a particular airline and its service agents, they are very likely to share their experiences with their friends and on social media. This creates a positive ripple effect on an airline's brand and reputation. Great customer service also plays a part in influencing customers' repurchase intentions and can be the deciding factor for customers who do not have a preference for any particular airline when planning their flights. Offering exceptional customer services allows airlines to:

- Turn complaints into opportunities
- Generate a positive impression
- Establish long-term relationship with customers
- Attract competitors' customers

On the other hand, if a customer is served badly, there will be negative repercussions.

AMBASSADORS VS. COMPLAINERS

An airline can turn customers into brand ambassador. Happy customers will recommend the airline to their relatives and friends, they will also write positive comments in forums and travel sites, and repurchase the airline's services.

On the other hand, unhappy customers can easily destroy an airline's reputation when they spread negative messages. In fact, the majority of customers do not make a formal complaint with an airline and instead, they will share their bad experiences with their friends, post them in forum, social media platform and blogs.

Both positive and negative posts can be spread rapidly online; customers can share their message online anytime at the check-in counter, boarding gate and even during a flight. People seem to be more interested in sharing negative posts as compared to positive ones and re-posting these messages allows the formation of public opinion on an airline. Those who have experience of a similar problem will then further elaborate the problem. In addition, when a customer posts a comment, reaction from the public is almost immediate. It is difficult for the customer to amend their post even though the airline service agent could resolve the problem later. Therefore, it is important for airline service agents to attend to customers' needs immediately.

Research has shown that positive posts spread faster than ones. An airline that provides excellent service can easily turn online feedback into a large marketing campaign as every sad post generates an extra 1.29 negative posts as compared to a normal post. On the other hand, every happy post has an even stronger impact: if a user posts an upbeat statement, an extra 1.75 positive posts are generated.[10]

> An incident at Chicago O'Hare airport took place on 10 April 2017 erupted in twitter, when a passenger was dragged out from an aircraft due to an overbooked flight.
>
> Another customer on a flight filmed and posted the incident on social media and within 2 days the video was shared over 100 thousand times. The news has also spread to other media including the traditional media all over the world.

SATISFIED CUSTOMERS VS. LOYAL CUSTOMERS

Satisfaction is a measurement used to evaluate whether an airline's performance exceeds the customers' expectations. Satisfied customers are created when customers are happy with the products and services provided by the airline.

Satisfied customers	Loyal customers
Created when normal expectations are met	The airline consistently solves their problems.
Will continue to purchase services until they find something better	Not easily attracted by competitors.
Basic needs are met	The airline consistently keeps its promises
No personal relationship formed	Trust developed
No personal interaction	Expect to be treated with extra respect
Will advertise mistakes to others	Promote the airline via word of mouth
Price sensitive	Not price sensitive
Functional transactions	Have higher expectations for their next trip
Sensitive to mistakes and problems	Understand and forgive minor mistakes made

Figure 1-12: Satisfied customers vs. loyal customers.

Loyal customers, on the other hand, are those who exhibit a devoted attitude towards airlines. Such behavior results in these customers making repeat purchases, rather than choosing the competing airlines. Loyalty is created when customers are continually satisfied with an airline's quality of service and products.

All airlines endeavor to meet their customers' basic expectations and to persuade satisfied customers to become loyal customers by offering additional services to increase and retain customer loyalty.

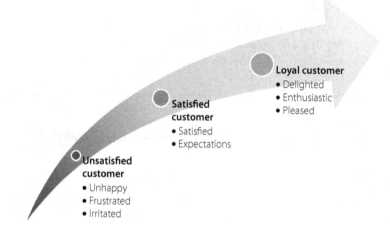

Figure 1-13: Shift from unsatisfied to loyal customer.

Statistics

Below are some facts and figures on customer satisfaction and loyalty, based on a study conducted by various US companies:

- It is 6 to 7 times costlier to attract a new customer than it is to retain an existing customer.[11]
- 54% of consumers shared bad experiences with more than 5 people, and 33% shared good experiences with more than 5 people.[12]
- 89% of consumers have stopped doing business with a company after experiencing poor customer service.[13]
- Consumers are 2 times more likely to share their bad customer service experiences than they are talking about positive experiences.[14]
- A 5% increase customer in retention increases profits by up to 95%.[15]

- For every customer who bothers to complain, 26 other customers remain silent.[16]
- More than 70% of buying experiences are based on how customers feel they are being treated.[17]

SUMMARY

Majority of today's airlines offer similar facilities on their flight. As such, they are competing with one another based on travel fare and the services offered. Excellent customer service is essential in securing customer repurchase intentions. Airlines use different strategies to turn satisfied customers to loyal customers so as to retain profitability.

APPLYING THE KNOWLEDGE

True or false?

Are the following statements true or false? Put a tick in the right column.

Statement	True	False
1. Customers are satisfied when their expectations are met.		
2. Service environment refers to the service landscape in which customers are in direct contact with airlines' products.		
3. Ambience refers to the social environment that influences customers' perception of an airline.		
4. Limited leg space between seats in an aircraft does not impact a customer's level of satisfaction.		
5. Deploying adequate service agents help to increase customers' level of satisfaction.		
6. Loyal customers make repeat purchases with an airline.		
7. Today's airlines are competing against one another based on customer service.		
8. When customers are happy with an environment, they have a tendency to stay put longer in the same location.		
9. Intangible customer service mainly focuses on service agents' abilities and skills in providing services.		
10. All customers are willing to pay more money for better services.		

Short-answer questions

1. How is customer satisfaction created in the airline industry? Explain your answer in full sentences.
2. What are the three elements make up the basics of minimum customer expectations?
3. How does a first-time flyer judge the quality of an airline? Explain your answer in full sentences.
4. What is customer service and why is it important to the airline industry? Explain your answer in full sentences.
5. Identify and explain the differences between an internal and external customer.
6. Write a list of the different characteristics of business and leisure customers.

ENDNOTES

1. Airbus. 2016. Commercial aviation accident 1958–2015. Airbus.
2. Karten, N. 1994. Managing Expectations: Working with People Who Want More, Better, Faster, Sooner, NOW!. Dorset house.
3. Lucas, R. 2011. Customer Service Skills for Success (Connect, Learn, Succeed). McGraw Hill.
4. Albert Mehrabian, James A. Russell An approach to environmental psychology Cambridge, Massachusetts: MIT Press, 1974.
5. Ghee, R. 2015 Mar 15. Creating a unique cabin environment—airlines investing in distinctive design and customer service. Future travel experience: http://www.futuretravelexperience.com/2015/03/creating-unique-cabin-environment-airlines-investing-distinctive-design-customer-service/
6. Bitner, M. 1992, Apr. Servicescapes: The Impact of Physical Surroundings on Customers and Employees. Journal of Marketing. Vol. 56, No. 2 pp. 57–71.
7. Flynn, D. 2015, Feb 12. Qantas to enforce dress code at Qantas Club airport lounges. Australian Business Traveller: http://www.ausbt.com.au/qantas-tightens-dress-code-at-qantas-club-airport-lounges

8. American Airlines. 2015. Conditions of Carriage. American Airlines: http://www.aa.com/i18n/customerService/customerCommitment/ conditionsOfCarriage.jsp#acceptanceofpassengers

9. Skyscanner. Bangkok to Hong Kong. http://www.skyscanner.co.th/routes/bkkt/ hkg/bangkok-to-hong-kong-international.html?langid=EN

10. Hall, Edward T. October (1963). A System for the Notation of Proxemic Behavior. American Anthropologist.

11. White House Office of Consumer Affairs Washington, DC.

12. Zendesk. 2013. The impact of customer service on customer lifetime value. Zendesk: https://www.zendesk.com/resources/ customer-service-and-lifetime-customer-value

13. Oracel. 2011. 2011 Customer Experience Impact Report. Oracel Cooperation: http://www.oracle.com/us/products/applications/cust-exp-impact-report-epss-1560493.pdf

14. American Express. 2012. 2012 Global Customer Service Barometer. American Express: http://about.americanexpress.com/news/docs/2012x/ axp_2012gcsb_us.pdf

15. Reichheld, F and Schefter, P. 2000. The Economics of E-Loyalty. Harvard business School: http://hbswk.hbs.edu/archive/1590.html

16. White House Office of Consumer Affairs Washington, DC.

17. Beaujean, M. Davidson, J and Medge, S. 2006. The 'moment of truth' in customer service. Mckinsey: http://www.mckinsey.com/insights/organization/ the_moment_of_truth_in_customer_service

CHAPTER TWO

Theory of Communication

Chapter Outline

Learning Objectives

After reading this chapter, the reader should be able to:

- Recognize the communication process
- Understand various communication barriers
- Recognize the importance of effective communication
- Identify different barriers to effective communication

COMMUNICATION IN THE AVIATION INDUSTRY

Communication is one of the important elements of customer service. Understanding customers' expectations and fulfilling their needs requires good communication skills. It is an act of transferring information from one person to another; many people consider communication the skill of talking and listening. However, effective involves other behavioral aspects. It is the art of transferring information both verbally and non-verbally and ensuring the content and the information delivered and received remain unchanged. Communications in the airline industry are in the form of interactions between airline frontline service agents and customers.

Communication process

The communication process consists of the various elements: sender, encoding, message, decoding, receiver, response, feedback, context and noise.

Sender

This refers to the person who initiates a message. His or her intention is to deliver a message to a specific audience and seek their response.

Encoding

To deliver the message, the sender needs to transform the message into a form that the receiver will understand. This process is known as encoding. The sender must evaluate the best method to ensure that the encoded message is understood by the receiver.

Receiver

This refers to recipient of the message.

Channel

The message is next delivered via the sender's desired channels of communication. The delivered message can be verbal or non-verbal and is usually transmitted via the various channels: face-to-face, handwritten formats, electronic mails, text messages and phone call conversations.

Decoding

After the message has been delivered, the receiver will need to decode the message and interpret it in a context that is understandable, whilst analyzing its meaning.

Response and feedback

After receiving the message, the receiver can choose to react with verbal or non-verbal responses or feedback. An example of a verbal response is a 'yes/no' reply and an example of a non-verbal response can be the mere nodding of one's head to indicate acknowledgement. The response is an action used by recipient to signal acknowledgment of receiving the message and feedback is the action taken by the receiver in response to the message received.

Context

It refers to the situation or location where the communication process takes place. The communication process may vary according to different locations and context. For example, one-on-one personal communication differs from communicating in groups as the content may be interpreted differently based on the context.

Noise

Communication noise is a barrier that influences the effectiveness of the communication process. Noise within the communication process

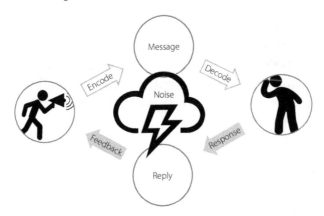

Figure 2-1: The communication process.

diverts the delivery of the message, leading it to be unable to be delivered successfully and the message may be misinterpreted, resulting in misunderstandings. These noise barriers may be created by machines, other background conversations and public announcements.

At the airport, a customer approaches the check-in counter.

Customer:
Excuse me; the self-check-in kiosk is not working.
I am unable to check in.

Ground Agent:
Madam, my apologies. I can help you with this
over here. Can I see your passport, please?
Breakdown of elements in the communication process
within this conversation:

Sender	Customer
Encoding	The customer has conveyed her experience with the kiosk machine through verbal speech.
Message	To inform the service agent that she is unable to check in
Decoding	The ground agent decoded the message and understood the problem.
Receiver	Ground agent
Response/ feedback	The ground agent replied by providing a solution and asking the customer to check in at the counter instead.
Context	Between the service user (customer) and the service provider (ground agent)
Noise	Potential background and environment noise at the check-in counter area include public announcements, other passengers' conversations and noise generated from nearby machines and equipment.

The arc of distortion

Joyce Osland et al (2006) explained that the arc of distortion model takes place when the sender's original intended message is interpreted entirely

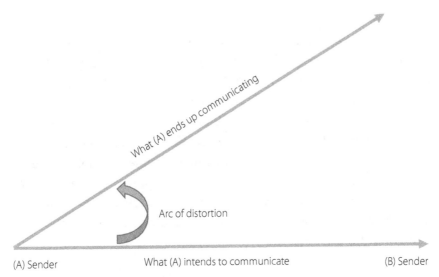

Figure 2-2: Arc of distortion.

differently by the receiver. This discrepancy occurs due to communication gaps. A communication gap occurs due to various reasons that cause the receiver to decode a different meaning of the actual message.[1]

When A (sender) is sending a message to B (receiver), the message may be understood in different ways due to the arc of distortion. The arc of distortion creates a communication gap containing various elements that results in ineffective communication. These elements are also known as the noises within the communication process that cause communication barriers.

Communication barriers

Dickson (1999) has defined several sources of noises. These noises create barriers to the effectiveness of the communication process.[2]

Psychological

The perceptual biases of the receiver often affect how a message is interpreted. Stereotyping often affects the delivery of the message as one individual judges another based on characteristics such as race, way of dressing and physical appearance. For example, one would usually assume that a customer who is wearing singlet, shorts and flip flops is taking economy class.

Semantic

The message can be distorted due to cultural differences and language barriers. Words, phases, signs and symbols may not be interpreted in the same way by people from different cultures. Words can have distinctive meanings in different contexts, time and situation. For example, the sentence "We saw her duck." can be interpreted as either to look at a duck that belongs to a woman or to look at someone squatting down quickly to avoid something. Another example is when a cabin crew asks a customer who is not familiar with the local cuisine to choose between chicken noodles or a vegetarian meal. The customer may assume that there are three choices to choose from: chicken, noodles and vegetarian.

Environmental

The environment can create communication barriers due to the factors present at the actual communication channels. These include the layout of the location, temperature and lighting among the others. For example, before the aircraft's final descent and landing, the purser will turn the cabin's lights to the brightest while alerting passengers to fasten their seat belts.

Demographics

Factors related to demographics such as age, gender and nationality can influence the way a message is interpreted. An individual may shake their head to demonstrate that they disagree about something while another of same nationality may do the same as a gesture of agreement. In addition, the nodding of one's head may be a universal sign of agreeing, it does not necessarily show approval.

Disability

Deafness, blindness or speech impairment are examples of physical disabilities that may cause communication barriers. External assistance may be needed in these instances to overcome these barriers in order for both the sender and the receiver to communicate effectively.

Organizational

The lack of communication between teams can also create a barrier to effective communication. For example, a customer seated in the first-class cabin told the cabin crew that he does not wish to be disturbed during meal time. However, the message was not conveyed clearly to the rest of the team and the customer became very upset when a serving member of the crew woke him up.

Eliminating barriers to communication
Clear and concise messages

Frontline service agents should always use simple sentences for efficient communication with customers, especially when dealing with complicated situations. This is to avoid any confusion and to ensure customers are able to follow the instructions and advices without any difficulty.

Customer: I have booked my ticket through a travel agent in March and they have confirmed that I am getting a window seat. This was also confirmed when I called to reserve my seats two days ago. It is not right for you to give my window seat away and give me an aisle seat. This is unacceptable!

Service agent: Mr. Smith, am I right to say that both your travel agent and our reservation agent have confirmed that you have been assigned a window seat?

The customer has raised several different issues in this conversation. The service agent immediately identifies the problem and addresses the customer's concerns.

Avoid using slangs or jargons

Slangs and jargons are widely used within the airline industry. These phases are used for service agents' own internal communication purposes and customers may not understand these terms. Misunderstanding and dissatisfaction can be created when service staff use slangs or jargons and this further confuses customers.

A flight is overbooked, and the airline is looking for passengers who are willing to give up their seats and board another flight.

Service agent: Excuse me, sir, we are looking for two DB customers. Can you help us?

Customer: I'm sorry but what are you talking about? I don't understand.

The term "DB" or "Denied Boarding" is widely used in the airline industry to refer to volunteers who give up their reservations in exchange for certain benefits. If an insufficient number of volunteers come forward to allow the remaining passengers to board the flight, the air carrier may then deny boarding to passengers against their will.

Whisper down the lane

When a message is delivered through many parties verbally, the message may sometimes be altered in the process. This is mostly seen within the airline internal communication when the top management relays new information and asks the manager to spread the information down the hierarchy. As service agents pass the message down from one to another, it may get distorted and the meaning of the original message may be completely altered. This can result in inaccurate rumors that cause misunderstandings and damage the company's reputation.

This can be avoided when the message is directly delivered to each receiver or sent out in a written format such as emails or text messages so as to minimize the chances of any potential effects of communication barriers.

At the check-in counter, the supervisor has informed a check-in service agent that "The flight to LAX is delayed for four hours, please give out a refreshment voucher to all passengers." This message is passed along the check-in counters and by the time it reached the last counter, the final message became "The flight to LAS is delayed for 14 hours, give out a one-night complimentary hotel stay."

Prejudging

Prejudging occurs when the receiver judges someone or something without going through all the facts. Airline service agents may assume that they already understand the customers' problem without any clarification, hence leading to inappropriate answers or decisions being made.

Two customers approach the check-in counter.

Customer: We would like to check-in.
Service agent: May I have your daughter and your passport, please?
Customer: Hey, who told you she was my daughter? She is my girlfriend.

The check-in service agent has prejudged the relationship of the customers according to their age and the customer was offended.

Cultural prejudices

This occurs when someone is judged according to their racial, cultural and religious group based on personal preference and experience. McLeod has defined prejudice an unjustified or incorrect attitude (usually negative) towards an individual based solely on the individual's membership of a social group.[3] For example, there is a stereotype that all African Americans are good at basketball and all Asians practices Kung Fu.

A Western customer is served by an Asian ground agent at the check-in counter.

Customer: Can you please help me to get someone who speak English?

The customer assumes that all Asians do not speak English.

EFFECTIVE COMMUNICATION

Even though modern technology has replaced many of the traditional communication channels, face-to-face communication is still the basis of servicing customers. Every day, airline service agents interact with customers at the airports and on aircrafts on a direct level. Face-to-face communication is not just limited to verbal conversation, it also includes non-verbal elements such as the tone of one's voice and body gestures. These three elements work together to ensure the message is delivered and that the level of customer service is maintained. On many occasions, customers prefer to talk to someone rather than communicate with a machine. The airline service agent can offer a much more personalized service, an aspect that machines are unable to replace. Effective communications include the effectiveness of how the message is delivered and received.

An effective message delivery

The objective of the sender is to ensure that the message is being understood. To confirm whether the message is delivered effectively, the sender should use appropriate wording, and the tone of voice and gestures help to facilitate the message delivery process.

Words

Face-to face-communication includes the use of words to deliver a message. The chosen words have a direct impact on the effectiveness of the communication. Using simple unambiguous words that are understood by the receiver is important. Avoid using jargons or slangs with the customers to avoid causing any confusion.

Message with jargons and slangs:
The flight is confronting severe turbulence; all passengers are expected to reappear to their allocated seats and have their seat belts secured.

Message that is worded in a simple manner:
We are now going through strong turbulence; all passengers are asked to return to your seats and have your seat belts fastened.

Tone of voice

One's tone also plays an important role in the message delivery process and affects how customers interpret a message. The tone of voice includes rate of speech and volume. If a service agent is speaking too fast, misunderstanding may occur as the customer may miss out some words and not receive the complete message. However, on the other hand, if the message is delivered at too slow a pace, it makes customers feel bored and disinterested in the conversation. The volume also impacts the content and delivery of the message as customers tend to perceive loud oral communication as impolite, whilst soft verbal communication may point to a service agent's lack of confidence and some information may be missed out.

Body gestures

Body language also impacts the effectiveness of the message being delivered. Body gestures that customers often notice include: facial expressions, whether the service agent is standing or sitting, eye contact and arm posture.

Smiling while delivering a message demonstrates happiness and customers will be more highly to accept the information. One's posture also forms a part of the message delivery process. Sitting up straight indicates that one is focused and paying attention to the conversation. Eye contact between service agents and the customers also indicates that one is paying attention. Looking at customers straight in the eye when they are speaking indicates that the service agent is giving them their undivided attention.[4] On the other hand, talking with one's arm crossed gives off an impression of negativity. It may indicate nervousness, which is either driven by a lack of trust in the other person or a general sense of discomfort.[5]

Words are sometimes not enough to convey a message as customers take other communication elements into consideration. According to Albert Mehrabia, professor emeritus of psychology, UCLA, research on communication has shown that:[6]

- 7% of meaning are in the words that are spoken
- 38% of meaning in words are paralinguistic (the way that the words are said)
- 55% of meaning in words are in facial expression.

Effective listening

Listening is one of the most important skills that all airlines' frontline service agent need to have as this is one attribute that not only affects their job effectiveness but also their relationship with other colleagues. Effective listening skills are a prerequisite in understanding customers' needs and demands, and resolve any issues that crop up.

Once they have interpreted the message, they then need to internalize and process the content before coming up with an appropriate response. Joseph DeVito (2000) explained that active listening consists of the following elements: receiving, understanding, remembering, evaluating, and responding.[7]

Receiving

Receiving refers to the intention of hearing one's message. The receiver's task is to filter out the unnecessary communication barriers such as noise and pick up the crux of the message. The receiver also needs to pay attention to the sender's facial expression and tone of voice when interpreting the message.

Understanding

The receiver then attempts to identify and "decode" the message. Due to various language barriers and cultural differences, the original meaning of the message may be perceived differently by the receiver. Based on this information, the receiver will process the information based on earlier related experiences.

Remembering

The receiver then needs to remember the message, or at least the important sections in order to follow up on it.

Evaluating

The receiver will evaluate the value of the message by using critical-thinking skills and determine whether it is important. Do they agree with the sender's point of view? Is the sender's argument logical? Are the requests reasonable?

Responding

After analyzing the message, the receiver then needs to respond accordingly. The receiver may choose to interpret the message or paraphrase it and reply to the sender to ensure it is received correctly. The receiver may also request for the sender to repeat the message verbally when he or she is confused.

According to Owen Hargie, the main purpose of listening includes the following:[8]

- Identify the message sent and the background noise from the surrounding environment
- Understand others' communication style
- Evaluate the message
- Identify the non-verbal signals
- Identify whether the receiver is paying attention to the sender
- Build relationship by showing care and concern
- Engage in a conversation, exchange information, debate on a topic and come up with an agreement.

Active listening skills

It is important to allow someone to finish conveying the entire message without any interruption. It is always a good practice to allow the speaker to finish the message before offering responses, and the listener should also remove all noise distractions. This can be done by stopping what they are doing and paying full attention to the speaker, and turning down the volume or turning off any devices which are sources of distraction.

It is also important that the listener demonstrates non-verbal communication techniques to indicate they are receiving the message and do not challenge what the speaker is saying even if they may not agree with the former. Non-verbal communication techniques include gestures such as maintaining eye contact and nodding one's head to show acknowledgement. These translate to the speaker that the listener shows interest in the conversation.

Evaluation should be only made after the complete message is received and the receiver should not demonstrate defensive actions at any point in time. Otherwise, the speaker will hesitate to continue the conversation. The listener is encouraged to ask questions when appropriate to clarify points that are ambiguous and to paraphrase the message whenever necessary to help in grasping and understanding the message. The listener may also pay attention to the speaker's facial and hand gestures so as to gauge the latter's feelings and emotions and to offer an appropriate feedback.

BARRIERS TO EFFECTIVE COMMUNICATION FOR AIRLINE SERVICE AGENTS

Speaking and listening related barrier results in the failure of the airline service agent to communicate with customers effectively. These barriers often cause confusion in which the airline service agent is either unable to communicate or ends up misinterpreting the customers' intentions.

Environmental barrier

The surrounding environment affects one's level of concentration. According to a study conducted in Cornell University, human performance is affected by the following environmental factors:[9]

- Temperature—The room is too hot or too cold.
- Brightness—The lighting is too bright or too dim.
- Sound—This includes noise and other disturbances.
- Air quality.
- Vibration.

The majority of the environmental factors are controlled by the airport, and frontline service agent will have to get used to these. In the aircraft cabin, some environmental factors may be adjusted by the cabin crew to help enhance their level of concentration whilst at work.

Linguistic barrier

The way that a message is delivered can be also a barrier to effective listening. In this instance, the use of difficult words, another language, slangs and jargons are barriers to listening that can create confusion.

The tone used, volume of speech and speed of talking are other linguistic barriers that airline service agents need to take into consideration.

Psychological barrier

The emotion of the receiver also pays a part in effective communication. When the recipient receives the information in a state of anger, frustration or when with prejudice, this often causes the original message to be perceived and interpreted differently.

Perceptual barrier

The receiver may sometimes regard the same situation from a different point of view due to differences in societal background, cultural background, and physical appearance. A culture that relegates female to a lesser position can also cause less effective communication.

Content barrier

The receiver may also lose their concentration when the subject of the message is not interesting or not related to them. The main point of the message may also be altered or diminished when the speaker talks for too long. Barriers are also created when the speaker repeats the same message too many times, causing the receiver to lose their level of concentration.

The Confusing Armagnac

An Asian customer is taking a business-class flight. After the meal, a customer called for the cabin crew.

Customer: Excuse me, can I please have an Armagnac?
Cabin crew: I am sorry, Mr. Wang, what do you need?
Customer: I would like an Armagnac. AR-MA-GNAC.
Cabin crew: One moment please, sir.

Several minutes later, the cabin crew returned with a senior cabin crew.

Senior cabin crew:	I am sorry, Mr. Wang. We cannot offer any medicine to the passengers.
Customer:	I am asking for Armagnac. Do you understand? AR-MA-GNAC.? A drink?
Senior cabin crew:	I am really sorry Mr. Wang. We thought you wanted an ān mián yào.

The pronunciation of sleeping pill in Chinese is "ān mián yào" and it sounds very similar to the beverage Armagnac. The cabin crew should have clarified with Mr. Wang right at the beginning by asking additional questions to avoid the awkward situation.

EFFECTIVE INTERNAL COMMUNICATIONS

Communication barrier may also be created during internal communications. On many occasions, the service agents are required to communicate with other internal staff through electronic devices such as a telephone or a walkie-talkie.

Communicating through electronic devices is much more difficult as compared to face-to-face communication as both the sender and the receiver are located in different locations and are very likely positioned in areas where there is environmental noise in the background. As such, the receiver needs to pay additional attention when listening to the message.

In this instance, one way of enhancing the effectiveness of internal communications is to use slangs and industry language.

SUMMARY

Communication is one of the most important elements within customer service. Understanding customers' expectations and fulfilling their needs require good communication skills. Even though modern technology is replacing many of the traditional communication channels, face-to-face communication still forms the basic communication channel in the service industry. There are times when speaking and listening barrier results lead to airline service agents failing communicate effectively with the customers. Hence, it is important for service agents to take a note of these barriers and improve on their existing communication skills.

APPLYING THE KNOWLEDGE

True or false?

Are the following statements true or false? Put a tick in the right column.

Statement	True	False
1. Communication is a process in which two or more elements of a system interact in order to achieve a desired outcome.		
2. Non-verbal communication is also known as communication without words.		
3. Verbal communication is often more effective than non-verbal communication.		
4. In the communication process, the sender's task is to decode the message.		
5. The sender's tone of voice and rate of speaking are content barriers that can cause confusion.		
6. One's appearance, facial expressions and inflection are part of written communication.		
7. Active listening requires rejecting messages based on one's personal value systems.		
8. The noise of aircraft engines is a likely source of environmental barrier.		
9. The arc of distortion model happens when the recipient receives a different message from the actual one that has been sent.		
10. It is most effective for service agents to use slangs or jargons when communicating with customers.		

Short-answer questions

1. Identify and explain all elements of the communication process.
2. What are the differences between verbal and non-verbal communication? List their advantages and disadvantages.
3. What are communication barriers and how can these barriers be eliminated? Explain your answers in full sentences.

4. How do environmental and linguistic barriers affect the performance of airline service staff?

5. Read the following scenario. What can cabin crew do to avoid the confusion in this situation due to the language barrier caused by different accents?

Cabin crew: How can I help you, madam?
Customer: I would like some water.
Cabin crew: Sure. One moment, please.

The cabin crew returns with a glass of water.
Customer: No. I want butter, not water.
Cabin crew: My apologies. One moment, please.

The cabin crew returns with some butter.
Cabin crew: Here you go, madam.
Customer: No ... no. I don't want butter. I am asking for vodka.
Cabin crew: My apologies, I'll be right back.

The customer returns with a glass of vodka.
Cabin crew: Here is your vodka, madam.
Customer: Thank you.

ENDNOTES

1. Osland, J. S. (2007). Organizational behavior: an experiential approach. Upper Saddle River: Pearson Prentice-Hall.

2. Dickson, D. (1999). Barriers to Communication. Interaction for Practice in Community Nursing, 84-132. doi:10.1007/978-1-349-14757-1_5

3. McLeod, S. (1970, Jan 01). Saul McLeod,: http://www.simplypsychology.org/prejudice.html

4. Skillyouneed.com. (2015). Non-Verbal Communication. Skillsyouneed.com: http://www.skillsyouneed.com/ips/nonverbal-communication.html

5. Changing minds. (2015). Arm body language. Changing mind: http://changingminds.org/techniques/body/parts_body_language/arm_body_language.htm

6. Mehrbabian, A. (1972). Nonverbal communication, Aldine Atherton, Chicago.

7. DeVito, J. A. (2000). The elements of public speaking (7th ed.). New York, NY: Longman.

8. Hargie, O. (2011). Skilled Interpersonal Interaction: Research, Theory, and Practice. London: Routledge, 182.

9. Hedge, A. (2004). Linking Environmental Conditions to Productivity, Cornell University.

CHAPTER THREE

The Basics of Customer Care

Chapter Outline

Chapter Outline

Learning Objectives

After reading this chapter, the reader should be able to:

- Recognize the role of airline frontline service agents
- Identify techniques of customer care
- Recognize frontline service agents' behavior
- Understand the importance of customer service language
- Understand the Karpman drama triangle

WHAT IS CUSTOMER CARE?

Customer care is one of the main duties of airline agents. It is the responsibility of airline frontline service agents, reservation agents, ground service agents and cabin crew to ensure passengers have a hassle-free experience by offering assistance, resolving their problems, and ensuring their safety throughout the journey. Every airline employee must understand their role and how he or she plays a part in affecting customers' travel experiences as they meet various airline personnel throughout their journey. It is equally important for all airline employees to understand the big picture of airline customers' satisfaction goal so that they can work together to achieve these common objectives as they carry out their daily work and interact with their respective internal and external customers.

To deliver excellent customer service, an airline must provide good quality and comparable tangible products. These include a reliable reservation system and check-in system, reliable baggage system, comfortable seats, tasty meals and in-flight entertainment. The airline also needs to ensure that frontline service employees provide high-quality service such as being knowledgeable, offer accurate information, demonstrate teamwork, have a positive attitude, are willing to take on responsibilities, possess excellent communicate skills and the ability to work under pressure.

How a product matches customers' expectations demonstrates its quality. Each customer has a unique set of expectations and therefore perceives quality differently.

The role of airline frontline service agents

The main responsibility of airline frontline service agents is to provide service to the customers among other roles to ensure the success of an airline's operation. To do so, frontline employees must be equipped with multiple skills to offer exceptional services to the customers.

Service provider

The main duty of service agents is to provide service and assistance to customers. A service agent must ensure that customers enjoy every single moment of the journey.

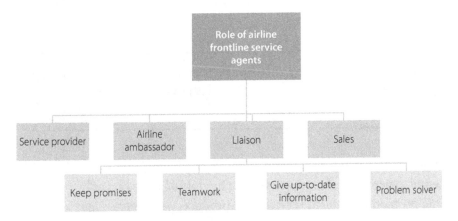

Figure 3-1: Different roles of airline frontline agents.

- Aim to satisfy the customers—generate happy customers by offering services
- Go the extra mile—perform beyond customers' expectations

> Mr. Yee is a frequent traveler who only takes window seats and the staff has assigned him to one before he arrived at the check-in counter. This has demonstrated their proactiveness in terms of satisfying customers' needs by going the extra mile. Even though customers may be satisfied when they are assigned to their desired seats during check-in, Mr. Yee was pleasantly surprised when he noted that his seat was prepared beforehand, hence creating a strong sense of satisfaction.

Airline ambassador

Service agents represent an airline through their words and actions.

- Being the brand of the airline—create the company's image
- First impression—create a positive impression at the first point of contact

Liaison

Service agents can also serve as middlemen by assisting customers to communicate with other airline departments when required.

- Help customers to contact the respective person or department to obtain proper assistance

> Mr. Yee was confused about his return flight as there was some discrepancy in the flight details. A staff assisted him to contact the travel agent for clarification.

Sales

Service agent may sometimes take on the role of a sales agent by offering and promoting in-flight services and products passengers might be interested in.

- Promote airlines' in-flight services and products
- Assist in increasing auxiliary revenue

> There was a special promotion for business class upgrades. The check-in staff noticed that Mr. Yee is a frequent traveler and suggested that he upgrades from economy to business class for a special price. Mr. Yee was very pleased to learn about this promotion and he agreed to do so.

Keep promises

This refers to service agents delivering services as guaranteed and ensuring what is promised to customers is carried out in a prompt manner.

> Even though a cabin staff was held up with several tasks on a full flight, she remembered the passengers' requests and fulfilled their needs. She ensured that all the promises made were kept.

Teamwork

Team spirit is important as individuals need to cooperate and work with colleagues and other airline service agents both within and across departments so as to achieve the airline's goal of building strong customer relationships.

- Help other team members—offer help to other colleagues when in need
- Everyone plays a part to ensure customers are satisfied with the entire journey

> The cabin crew is serving meals on both sides of a wide-body aircraft. Mr. Yee is seated on the last row. After he has been served, a cabin staff noticed that her colleague on the other side of the aisle was still halfway through the service. She immediately went over to help her colleague out.

Give up-to-date information

One of the main duties of a service agent is to deliver updated and accurate information to customers.

It is Mr. Yee's first trip to Sydney. He asked a staff about the arrival process upon landing in Sydney Airport. The staff explained the immigration and quarantine procedures to him in details.

Problem solver

Service agents also help customers in terms of resolving problems. During times of irregular operations, service agents offer the following:

- Give passengers advice that is in their best interest
- Offer solutions to problems by identifying multiple solutions and allowing customers to select what best fit their needs and offering a feasible solution after weighing out an airline's incurred cost and customers' benefits.

There was an unexpected flight delay. Mr. Yee had a choice of standing by for the next flight or getting a confirmed reservation on another that flight that departs in seven hours. Based on the situation, the staff recommended that he opt to standby for the subsequent flight while holding a confirmed seat on the other one flying out seven hours later to ensure Mr. Yee will be able to secure a flight back home.

Job rotation programs

Some airlines have implemented job rotation programs in order to achieve customer satisfaction goals. These programs allow service personnel to work in various environments and gain experience in different departments. This system helps them to increase their knowledge of the airlines' product so as to better address customers' problems on the spot, provide prompt services as well as gain in-depth understanding of customers' needs at different stages of the air travel process. For example, service agents who are based in the airports undergo a job rotation program whereby they are required to work in different functions such as ticketing, check-in, boarding and arrival.

Job rotation motivates service agents by offering them new challenges and the chance to learn new skills. It also helps to improve communication between departments and for staff to better understand the roles and functions of other departments. Moreover, this increases job mobility as staff who are equipped with multiple skills will be able to take over their colleagues' tasks in events of an emergency.

Studies have also shown that job rotation leads to increased employees' motivation and job satisfaction[1] as they become more familiar with their jobs and are more confident when communicating with customers.

From corporate culture to service culture

The corporate culture of an airline has a direct influence on frontline employees' behavior and overall performance as it shapes the way they interact with customers. Southwest Airlines, the world's largest low-cost carrier is famous for its corporate culture, which is also the driving factor for the airline's success. The company cares about its employees and seeks to create a favorable workplace for all individuals regardless of their roles. In turn, this is translated into the service culture of the company as employees are motivated to treat their customers in the same manner. When employees are satisfied with a company and their jobs, they are motivated to go the extra mile to ensure customer's needs are fulfilled and that they enjoy the airlines' products and services.

The Southwest Airlines Culture

Southwest Airlines' corporate culture focuses on every person in the company. This includes its employees and the customers. This business strategy has resulted in Southwest bagging the 7th position of *Fortune's* World's Most Admired Companies.[2] Southwest Airlines success is based on the formula "Happy Employees = Happy Customers = Increased Business/ Profits = Happy Shareholders!"[3]

Southwest Airlines' Mission[4]

The mission of Southwest Airlines is dedication to the highest quality of Customer Service delivered with a sense of warmth, friendliness, individual pride, and Company Spirit.

Commitment to Employees

We are committed to provide our Employees a stable work environment with equal opportunity for learning and personal growth. Creativity and innovation are encouraged for improving the effectiveness of Southwest Airlines. Above all, employees will be provided the same concern, respect, and caring attitude within the organization that they are expected to share externally with every Southwest Customer.

Putting People First—British Airways

In 1983, the chief executive officer (CEO) of British Airways, Colin Marshall launched the "Putting People First" program to improve the company's customer service.[5] His objectives were to improve the company culture by increasing employees' awareness of teamwork and the importance of every individual's role in contributing to the company's success.

Value of caring

The basic element of caring is to help and show concern to others. Caring for and offering assistance to others is driven by deep value-based motivations and efforts to make a positive and practical difference to their lives. In the airline industry, frontline service agents offer care and concern to passengers to ensure every customer is satisfied with the travel experience. The principles of caring include the following:

Acknowledge the actual boss	There will be no airlines without customers. They are the real bosses of all airline service agents.
Maintain customers	Create satisfaction by offering excellent services to customers as to achieve high customer retention.
Value the relationship created with customers	It takes a lot of time and effort to establish a great relationship with customers. All airline service agents should endeavor to maintain it.
Go the extra mile by doing more than expected.	Performing beyond customers' expectations will greatly increase their satisfaction level.

| Treat others how you want to be treated | Service agents should put themselves in the shoes of the customers and think about how they would like to be treated. This is the minimal quality of service they are expecting. |
| Treat your customer as you would treat as your friend | Think about what you would do if you value a friendship. Frontline service agents should apply the same to their customers. |

The goal of caring

The main goal of airline frontline service agents is to ensure a smooth and comfortable travel experience for passengers. This helps airlines to establish strong relationships with customers and achieve high customer retention.

Customers tend to only remember outstanding services. That said, excellent service sometime can be very simple, such as in the instance of a service agent recalling the customer's name, or remembering the customer's

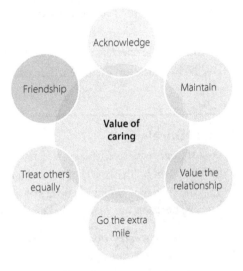

Figure 3-2: The value of caring.

seating and meal preferences. These satisfied customers then become return customers and refer or share their experience with their friends, and post positive reviews on web forums and on social media.

IMPORTANCE OF ETHICS

Service agents should also consider the ethics involved when making a decision. Ethic values refer to a set of established principles that govern behavior and usually determine what is right and wrong. In order to help ensure that a good reputation is maintained, many companies usually set some standard ethic values for airline staff to abide by when interacting with customers. These values help the airline to build customer trust and generate loyal customers. Below are some questions that service agents can ask themselves when facing a situation that calls for them to make an ethical decision.

- Am I doing anything that is against the law?
- Is this violating any safety measure?
- Is the decision made fair to all other passengers?
- What will be the reaction of other customers when they know about this?
- What will be the reaction of other staff when they know about this?
- Will this decision create further problems?

Is it ethical?

A customer requested to carry a 15 kg baggage on board the aircraft. The service agent politely rejected the customer's requests even though she knew that the customer would not be happy about it.

The decision was made based on the following considerations:

- Overweight carry-on baggage could create a safety hazard in the cabin. It could cause serious injury if the baggage fell out from the overhead bin.
- It is not fair to other passengers who have made similar requests and were rejected.
- How the other passengers who have made similar requests would react if they learned about this and its impact on the company's image.
- The need for fair and consistent treatment of all passengers.
- What should be done if the customer makes a similar request next time when he travels? Should the company's policy be changed to accommodate such requests?

CUSTOMER CARE TECHNIQUES

Customers have different needs and levels of expectation. The role of a frontline service agent is to identify these different types of passengers especially those who require additional assistance. This includes passengers with disabilities, pregnant individuals, unaccompanied minors and the elderly.

Each customer is an individual

Even though airline service agents need to interact with hundreds of customers every day, it is vital to treat each passenger as a special individual. This means service agents need to understand the customers and perform all necessary tasks to fulfill their needs.

Address customers by title and name

- Personalized service can be demonstrated by addressing customers by name. Before obtaining a customer's last name, frontline service agents can address them using "sir" or "madam". However, when customers' last names are made available, service agents should always address them by their last names, i.e. "Mr. Jones", "Ms. Chan" as a sign of respect. Whenever possible, always address customers by their title, followed by their last name. The figure below shows some examples:
- Mister refers to a male customer and its written abbreviation is Mr.
- Mistress is used for married females and its written abbreviation is Mrs.
- Miss is used for females whose marriage status is unknown.
- Doctor is used for an academia who achieved doctorate-level degree and its written abbreviation is Dr.
- Father is used for a priest.
- Sister is used for a nun.
- Holiness insured to address a Buddhist Monk.

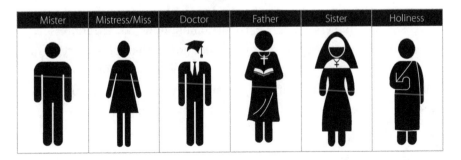

Figure 3-3: Customers' title.

"Good Afternoon, Sir."

A customer approaches the check-in counter.

Service agent: Good afternoon, sir. How are you today?

Customer: I am fine, thank you. I would like to check in for my flight to Sapporo

Service agent: Certainly, sir. May I have your passport, please?

Customer: Here you go.

Service agent: Thank you, Mr. Smith. Can I confirm that your final destination for today is Sapporo?

Customer: I am Dr. Smith. Yes, I am going to Sapporo.

Service agent: Mr. Smith ... Oh, I am sorry. Dr. Smith, do you have any bags to check in?

Customer: No bags.

Service agent: Mr. Smith, would you like a ....

Customer: How many times do I need to tell you to address me as Dr. Smith?

Service agent: I am sorry. Dr. Smith. Would you like a seat by the window or aisle?

Customer: Aisle.

Service agent: Dr. Smith, here is your boarding pass to Sapporo with seat number, 45C. The boarding gate is 4A. Please be at the gate at least 20 minutes before flight departures. Thank you.

As some customers are very particular about how they are addressed, it is important for service agents to pay attention to their preferences. This case study above is an example which check-in agents should inform their colleagues located at the boarding gate and the cabin crew to ensure that they address the customer using the right title at all times.

UNDERSTANDING THE BASICS

Even though frontline service agents may only interact with customers for a few minutes at the airport, a pleasant and hassle-free experience will determine how they feel about an airline and its representatives. Airline

Do the		Thing
At the	**RIGHT**	Time
Respond with		Actions
Using the		Attitude

Figure 3-4: How to create customer satisfaction.

service agents can create satisfied customers by following the simple rules of doing the right thing at the right time and responding with the right action and a right attitude.

Behavior

It is important for frontline service agents to put their emotions aside while they are on duty and treat all customers in the same manner. This is because negative emotions can often result one's behavior and attitude. It is also crucial that they maintain a professional front and positive attitude even when dealing with unreasonable customers, and help them to resolve difficult situations regardless of their behavior.

Interaction skills

Today, many companies are training their frontline customer service agents with basic communication skills to help them manage their emotions when dealing with unpleasant situations.

Providing good customer service is akin to being an actor. According to David Evans, chairman of Grass Roots, a company specializing in employee solutions and customer engagement, you are only as good as your last performance.[6]

To maintain professionalism, frontline service agents are required to put on a front stage mask to demonstrate friendliness and show concern even when interacting with demanding customers as it is inappropriate for service agents to show any signs of annoyance. As such, basic acting skills can help service agents to remain calm and continue their duties professionally. This is also known as dramaturgy.

Figure 3-5: Service agents need to put on a face mask while on duty.

Dramaturgy refers to a change of a person's behavior dramaturgical due to the differences in time, place, and audience.[7] Based on the theory and practice of dramatic composition, a person has a front stage and a back stage. The front stage (behavior) of a person will change according to the changes in the environment and the audience while the back stage (true personality) of the person is hidden.

An example is an agent who is on duty at the check-in counter. Even though the agent encounters a rude passenger, he maintains his front stage and continues to serve the customer in a friendly manner. During break time, he reveals his back stage he complains about the rude customer's behavior to the other agents.

In view of such situations, frontline service agents must be equipped with cognitive skills that allow them to make adjustments to the way they deal with customers, and according to the situation without compromising on the service quality.[8]

Appearance

This is the first thing customers notice about service agents and this becomes one of the first criteria used to evaluate their level of professionalism. As such, airline frontline employees are required to wear uniforms in order to demonstrate an airline's brand and professionalism. In addition, service agents are required to put on a well-groomed and presentable front. This includes maintaining neat and tidy overall appearance, ironed uniforms and polished shoes.

Communication

Communication barrier may sometimes be created due to accents. As such, frontline service agents should pay extra attention to their pronunciation.

Tone of voice

Different tones of voice are used according to the type of customers served and based to the different situations. For example,

Figure 3-6: Approachable gesture vs not approachable gesture.

the tone of one speaking to elderly passengers will not be the same as with a teenager.

Body language

Service agents should use a variety of body language to facilitate the conversation, and keep their arms uncrossed and palms open to show acceptance. They also need to maintain eye to demonstrate attentiveness, and sit upright when attending to customers to show readiness. In addition, service agents should refrain from touching their face or hair while serving customers as it demonstrates boredom and lack of attentiveness.

Facial expression

Service agents should not show any sign of anger even in face of unreasonable and demanding situations. Instead, they need to maintain their smile and a positive attitude throughout.

CUSTOMER SERVICE ATTRIBUTES

Customer service plays an important role in generating customers' satisfaction, and employers are constantly on the lookout for the following attributes when hiring potential customer service employees: approachability, level of observance, ability to understand others, attentiveness, communication skills and response time.

Approachability

Someone who is approachable is responsive, open and ready to assist others. It is an essential aspect of professional customer service and plays a vital role in customers' overall experience when interacting with service agents. One's level of approachability is usually determined based on three elements: attitude, reliability and standard of service.

Attitude

Before customers approach a service agent for assistance, they will often gauge their gestures and facial expressions from a distance. These include

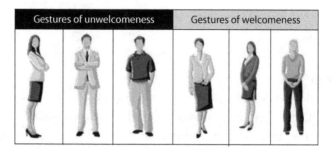

Gestures of unwelcomeness	Gestures of welcomeness

Figure 3-7: Gestures demonstrating hospitality.

weighing their gestures and facial expressions, such as the way they stand and the placement of their arms.

Standing in a welcoming position with one's arms open demonstrates friendliness and attentiveness. On the other hand, standing and leaning on something with crossed arms or placing one's hands in the pockets may signal unwelcomeness or even hostility.

Reliability

Reliability is generated when customers have access to the services they need or expect. By the time they arrive at the airport, they expect to be served as soon as possible, and the availability of service agents at the various locations demonstrates this quality. Trust is also gained when customers have confidence in the security and confidence of an airline.

Flexibility

Most airlines usually allow service agents to make minor adjustments to products and services so as to cater to the various customers' needs. As such, it is important for service agents to identify the different types of customers whilst ensuring the company's policy is not violated.

Observant and understanding towards others

While not everyone has the knack for observing others' needs, this is an attribute that can be developed through experience. Strong observation skills allow service agents to read customers' mind. This gives them insight into customers' minds and helps them to predict their needs. Service agents are encouraged to take note of how other airlines provide services and adopt their best practices.

Cues such as observing customers' gestures, facial expressions and tone of voice provide information about their mood, patience level and even their personality. These help service agents to ensure positive interactions with customers.

> The ground service agent senses that something was amiss when a customer approaches him for assistance at the baggage belt area. The customer explains that he has just received a phone call about a death in his family and needs to return home immediately.
>
> Upon noting the customer's frantic expression, the service agent can help him to calm him down by providing the following:
>
> - Ask the customer for his baggage receipt and passport in order to help to retrieve his baggage. This gives the customer time to make all other necessary arrangements for the flight back.
> - Check the earliest available flight
> - Check if the customer has a return ticket and the possibility of changing the date of departure
> - If the customer does not have a return ticket, offer several options such as discount ticket and mileage redemption ticket.
> - Help the customer to get the ticket ready and assist him to check in for the return flight

There are instances whereby customers do not state their demands and requests explicitly. It then falls upon agents to observe and interpret the true meaning behind customers' comments and feedback. Below are some examples:

Customers' comment	Possible actual feedback and/or request
"My legs hurt."	"Can I have another seat with more leg space?"
"There seems to be a long queue today."	"The waiting time is too long."
"The check-in process seems complicated."	"The service agent is too slow."
"The food tastes bland."	"The food does not taste good."

Attentiveness

Paying attention to customers allows service agents to be more focus on the customers' needs. William James, an American philosopher and psychologist, came up with the Spotlight model, which views attention as being like a torch that has a central focus, a margin and a fringe. This is based on the rationale

Figure 3-8: Putting customers under the spotlight.

that we can pay attention to things without pointing at them such as in the example of noticing someone without explicitly staring at them. Attention can also be in the form of a broad light, in the instance of a motorist spreading his attention in take in all the movement and traffic around him.[9] Just like a motorist, service agents should pay attention to customers' needs whilst taking in the surrounding environment and other external factors into consideration, without being distracted by them. In instances when large groups of customers check in at the same time, service agents will need to adjust themselves by giving equal attention to all customers. Service agents should not be distracted while serving customers as this is a sign of disrespect. When in face of urgent matters, service agents should always ask for permission from customers they are currently serving to attend to other immediate requests before getting back to them.

Clear communication

Service agents need to deliver messages in a clear and precise manner, and using the correct wording and tone of voice will create an impression of helpfulness. As customers expect their queries to be answered promptly, it is important for service agents to understand their problem in the shortest time possible and to give a straightforward response.

On many occasions, service agents are given very limited time to respond to a query and they must think quickly, put the message into the most appropriate wording and reply in the correct tone of voice. Service agents must also be confident in their response as customers will pay attention to their choice of words and tone of voice during the interaction.

K.I.S.S   **Keep it simple and short**

Communication skills

It takes listening skills, analysis skills and message transmission skills to deliver a message to a customer. The main goal of service agents is to ensure that the message is delivered successfully and that there is no room for doubt in the message. As such, it is important for service agents to have excellent communication skills so that they are able to communicate with customers using a mix of both verbal and non-verbal communication strategies to ensure the message is transmitted successfully.

A lounge service attendant approached Mr. Lee at the business lounge. "Mr. Lee, your flight is ready for boarding." Mr. Lee nodded in acknowledgement as he was focusing on replying to emails on his laptop.

Ten minutes later, the service attendant approached Mr. Lee again. "Mr. Lee, you should board the flight now." Mr. Lee replied. "Sure. Give me a minute. I am almost finished with my email," and continued working on his laptop. Ten minutes later, the service attendant reminded Mr. Lee again, "Mr. Lee, you need to board your flight now." By the time Mr. Lee arrived at the boarding gate, the flight had already left.

While the lounge service agent had already informed Mr. Lee, there was a communication breakdown because the customer was so focused on his work that he did not receive the message. At the same time, the service agent failed to check with Mr. Lee to ensure he understood the message, hence causing the customer disservice.

Responsiveness

Response and resolution times are equally important factors in determining customer satisfaction. Service agents must be quick-thinking and be able to provide solutions in the shortest time possible. While most customers can tolerate some mistakes, the failure to respond quickly to problems can often affect an airline's reputation. Service agents must also be prepared to deal with unusual scenarios where the best solution to the problem is not included in the company's guidelines. Being responsive also means being proactive in terms of solving customers' problems, diffusing possible tense situations, or even going the extra mile to impress and surprise customers with unexpected acts of gestures. These are the factors that distinguish the quality of service.

Patience

Being patient and spending the time and effort to understand customers' requests and problems allow service agents to offer the best solutions. In instances whereby customers show signs of confusion or frustration, demonstrating patience helps to calm them down.

Smart phone addiction

Spending time on a smartphone may seem a normal part of today's smartphone addicted culture. Some service agents are guilty of the same as they are focused on their smartphones and are unaware of the customers standing in front of them.

In such cases, customers will often feel that these agents are not ready or unwilling to serve them. They may also be hesitant to approach service agents who are using their phones for fear of disturbing them.

Service agent should refrain from personal usage of mobile device while serving customers. When service agents are using mobile devices for work purposes, it is important to engage in a conversation and maintain eye contact with customers whenever possible. This will minimize any misunderstanding of disservice.

THE LANGUAGE OF CUSTOMER SERVICE

Service agents need to communicate verbally with customers and the use of certain words and phrases will help to convey a sense of courteousness.

Greetings

Greetings are used to welcome customers and when greeting them for the first time. It also implies that service agents acknowledge the customers' presence.

Sample greeting messages:

- "Hello."
- "Hello, how are you?"
- "Good morning/afternoon/evening, how are you?"

Welcome messages

Welcome messages are used by service agents when customers arrive at the airlines' premises. These include an airline's check-in area, boarding gate area, airline lounge and the aircraft. A welcome message can also be made via the public announcement system at the boarding gate and in the aircraft cabin.

Sample welcome messages:

- "Welcome to C&M Airline."
- "Welcome to the business class lounge."
- "Welcome on board."
- "Welcome back." (for return customers)

Gratitude messages

Gratitude messages are used to show gratefulness and politeness.

Sample gratitude messages:

- "Thank you."
- "Thank you very much."
- "Thank you, sir/madam."

- "Thank you for flying with C&M Airline."
- "Thank you for your cooperation." (when customers comply with service agents' instructions)

"Please" messages

These are usually used when service agents pose a request to customers. The imperative word "please" can be used in a variety of context.

Sample "please" messages:

- "Please have your boarding pass ready for boarding."
- "Can you please pass me the food tray?"
- "Please fasten your seat belt."
- "Can I have your boarding pass, please?"

Inquiry messages

Inquiry messages are used when service agents require customers to make a decision. Open inquiry messages give customers the option to freely state their preferences while close inquiry messages require customers to choose from a limited set of options available.

Sample open inquiry messages:

- "Where would you like to be seated?"
- "What you like to drink, sir?'
- "What would you like to have for dinner?"

Sample closed inquiry messages:

- "Would you like a window seat at the front or an aisle seat at the rear of the aircraft?"
- "Would you like some orange juice or apple juice?"
- "What would you like for dinner? Chicken congee or beef noodles?"

Well wishes

Well wishes and pleasantries are often used just before goodbye messages.

> Sample well-wishing messages:
>
> - "We wish you a nice flight."
> - "Have a great journey."

Goodbye messages

Goodbye messages are used at the end of an interaction with customers.

> Sample goodbye messages:
>
> - "Goodbye, sir."
> - "We hope to see you again, goodbye."

Rejection messages

Messages of rejections are used when service agents are unable to fulfill customers' demands. The usage of the word "no" is prohibited in the service industry as it demonstrates impoliteness. As such, service agents use different phrases to decline customers' requests.

> Sample rejection massages:
>
> - "I am afraid your preferred seat is unavailable."
> - "I am unable to meet your requests."

Apologies

Apologies are used when airline or service agents are unable to deliver as promised. Apologies can be used together with "please" messages when seeking for customers' forgiveness.

Sample apologies:

- "I am sorry, sir. The flight has been delayed."
- "My apologies for what had happened earlier."
- "I would like to apologize for the flight cancellation on behalf of the company."
- "Please accept our sincere apologies."

SOCIAL DISTANCE

Social distance is a measure of social separation caused by perceived or real differences between groups of people as defined by well-known social categories. It manifests across a variety of social categories, including class, race and ethnicity, culture, nationality, religion, gender and sexuality, and age, among others.

In the service industry, social distance is a factor that influences the effectiveness of communication between

Figure 3-9: Social distance.

service agents and customers. Social distance helps to create an atmosphere for a more comfortable interaction between people of different degrees of closeness. According to Edward Hall, an American anthropologist and cross-cultural researcher, the rule of social distance between two people is classified into the following four zones: public, social, personal, and intimate.[10]

The public zone refers to a distance of 3 meters or more between two individuals. Most people will choose to stand slightly away from those they do not know on a personal basis. For example, at the check-in counter, customers will not stand very closely together when queuing to check in. Most people tend to feel safe and a sense of privacy when there is adequate distance separating them.

The social zone refers to a distance of 1.5 meters to 3 meters between two persons. This allows two individuals to communicate verbally while keeping a safe distance. This is a comfortable distance for a formal interaction between people who do not know each other.

The personal zone is the distance of 0.5 meter to 1.5 meters between two persons. This is a good distance for effective direct communication. One usually allows another to enter their personal zone when trust and friendship is developed.

The intimate zone refers to a distance of 0.5 meter or less between two individuals. More often than not, one only allows another to enter their intimate zone if they know them very well, such as the instance of family members.

In airline customer service, it is unprofessional for service agents and customers to be in the public and intimate zones. Calling out to customers from a distance is impolite while standing too close to customers creates discomfort. The recommended interaction distance between service agents and customers is between 0.5 and 3 meters, i.e. the social zone or personal zone. The majority of customers feel more comfortable when they are interacting with service agents within the social zone while frequent travelers who are well-acquainted with certain service agents usually prefer to interact at the personal zone.

CREATING HAPPY CUSTOMERS

Putting effort into minute details can bring about high customer satisfaction. Happy customers can be created when service agents paying attention to the following details:

- Include a personal touch through addressing customers by their names
- Offer additional assistance to the customers with disability
- Use the common queue method to reduce customers' waiting time at check-in counters
- Speed up the boarding process by boarding customers in batches
- Offer personalized services

Protected under the sun

Trang is a small airport located in the southern part of Thailand. The airport only has two remote parking areas and airline passengers are required to walk on the tarmac that links the aircraft and the passenger terminal building during boarding and disembarking. Nok Air is an airline operating flights from this airport. In view of the airport's layout, the airline offers umbrellas to passengers while boarding to shelter them from the sun and rain. More often than not, it is these small details that win over customers.

THE KARPMAN DRAMA TRIANGLE

In the early 1970s, Steven Karpman, a psychiatrist, came up with the Karpman drama triangle model to explain the types of interactions that take place between people during a conflict. The model was created based on Eric Berne's transaction analysis model in the 50s which claims that individuals' interactions are motivated by their social settings and environment.[11]

According to the Karpman drama triangle, the general population takes on the three primary roles of persecutor, victim and rescuer when interacting with others.

Persecutor

The persecutor is someone who holds power. Persecutors are controlling, serious, oppressive, aggressive, commanding, inflexible, and consider themselves to be more superior than others. A persecutor needs to be in control and often uses verbal or physical power to stay in authority.

They believe that they are always right and when caught in a conflict, they are the ones that usually look for reasons to prove that others are wrong.

Victim

Also known as the persecuted, the victim is seen as helpless, discouraging, weak, guilty, and unable to make decisions or solve problems. Such individuals have the tendency to give up easily and lose their ground when they are challenged by others. They also display a lack of self-confidence and may exhibit passive-aggressive behavior.

Rescuer

A drama triangle situation is created when two individuals interact and one is seeking assistance from another. In this case, the rescuer is the character who "rescues" those whom they regard as vulnerable.

The role of these individuals can either remain unchanged or be switched during an interaction.

Figure 3-10: The Karpman drama triangle.

In the context of the airline service industry, customer service agents usually take on the role of a rescuer when they offer assistance to customers (the victims). However, some customers may unknowingly become persecutors when they make unreasonable demands.

The following is an example:

A customer (victim) approaches the service agent (rescuer).

Customer: Hi. I would like to change my seat number because I don't like window seats.

Service agent: Sure, I can help you to change your seat.

The customer and service agent have now established their roles as victim and rescuer in the triangle. Subsequently, the service agent informed the customer that he was unable to change the seat number as the flight was fully booked.

Service agent: I am sorry, sir. The flight is full. As such, I am unable to change your seat number.

Customer: What? You just said earlier that you can help me. You cannot even perform a simple task. You are not being helpful at all. I want to talk to your supervisor.

The customer then lost his temper and took on the role of the persecutor as he started yelling at the service agent (victim). The service agent's supervisor was informed about the situation immediately.

Supervisor: Hello sir, my colleague has told me that you would like to have your seat changed.

Customer: Yes, your service agent has promised to change my seat and he is unable to do it. This is ridiculous.

During the conversation with the supervisor (rescuer), the customer has yet again, changed his role to that of a victim. The supervisor eventually managed to change the customer's seat and their roles switched once again.

Supervisor: I apologize for what happened earlier. Here is your new seat assignment.

Customer: Thank you. I hope your agent will learn from this and improve on his customer service skills. He should not have promised on something that he could not deliver.

Now the supervisor has become the victim while the customer is the rescuer.

Staying out of the triangle

All service agents should try to stay out of the drama triangle so as to avoid becoming a victim and getting personal complaints from customers. Below are several ways service agents can keep themselves out of such situations:

- Only make promises that they can deliver
- Take responsibility for their own actions
- Do not engage in a confrontation with customers
- Do not be defensive
- Do not attack others
- Always take a deep breath and calm down when facing potential scenarios of conflict

Think of a situation where you have been a rescuer, victim or persecutor. You might even have played all three roles in one situation!

SUMMARY

The responsibilities of airline frontline service agents are to ensure a hassle-free experience for the passengers by offering assistance, resolving their problems, and ensuring their safety throughout the journey. As airline representatives, service agents are evaluated based on a number of factors. These include approachability, attitude, reliability, flexibility, attentiveness, communication skills and responsiveness.

It is important for service agents to adjust and adapt themselves to ensure that all customers are satisfied without compromising the company's policy. The most successful customer service transaction is to turn a complaining customer to a brand ambassador.

In conclusion, the Karpman drama triangle model explains the types of interactions that take place between the persecutor, victim and rescuer during a conflict.

APPLYING THE KNOWLEDGE

True or false?

Are the following statements true or false? Put a tick in the right column.

Statement	True	False
1. A service agent is an airline representative that offers service to the customer on the airline's behalf.		
2. Service agents' behaviors are influenced by an airline's corporate culture.		
3. A customer evaluates the professionalism of an airline service agent from the very first moment they have a conversation.		
4. Keeping one's arms crossed is a sign of welcomeness.		
5. A successfully delivered message involves a combination of listening skills, analysis skills and translation skills.		
6. Customers expect service agents to take their time to solve their problems.		
7. Strong customer relationships are established when service agents are able to understand customers' feelings.		
8. The public zone refers to the least amount of distance between two people.		
9. Paying attention to small details help to drive customers' satisfaction.		
10. When caught in a conflict, service agents should strive to come up with a solution to achieve a win-lose situation in order please customers.		

Short-answer questions

1. Identify and explain the reasons for a customer complaint.
2. What does the phrase "attending small detail drives customer satisfaction" mean? Explain your answer in full sentences.
3. How are happy customers created? Explain your answer in full sentences.
4. Explain the importance of service language and give an example for each of the following customer service language:
   a. Greetings
   b. Welcome messages
   c. Gratitude messages
   d. "Please" messages
   e. Inquiry messages

f. Goodbye messages
g. Well wishes
h. Rejection messages
i. Apologies

ENDNOTES

1. Plowman, N. (2010 Dec 6). Advantages of Job Rotation: Reduce Turnover by Influencing Employee Burnout, Satisfaction, and Motivation. Bright hub: http://www.brighthub.com/office/entrepreneurs/articles/55274.aspx

2. Fortune. (2015). World's Most Admired Companies 2015. Fortune: http://fortune.com/worlds-most-admired-companies/southwest-airlines-7/

3. Southwest. (2011, Mar 11). Southwest Airlines "Gets It" With Our Culture. Southwest blog http://www.blogsouthwest.com/southwest-airlines-%E2%80%9Cgets-it%E2%80%9D-our-culture/#sthash.FdV3eRMG.dpuf

4. Southwest. (2015). About Southwest. Southwest Airlines: https://www.southwest.com/html/about-southwest/

5. Calder, S. (2012, JUL, 6). Lord Marshall: Executive who turned British Airways from a sleeping giant into a world leader. Independent: http://www.independent.co.uk/news/obituaries/lord-marshall-executive-who-turned-british-airways-from-a-sleeping-giant-into-a-world-leader-7920614.html

6. Edwards, B. (2010). A useful guide to customer service. Pansophix.

7. George Ritzer. (2007). Contemporary Sociological Theory and Its Classical Roots: The Basics. New York, New York. McGraw-Hill.

8. Korz, R. (2003). Service Engineering: A Multidisciplinary Approach, Books on demand GmbH, Germany.

9. Eriksen, C; Hoffman, J. (1972). "Temporal and spatial characteristics of selective encoding from visual displays". Perception & Psychophysics.

10. BBC NEWS. (2014 Mar 13). Study: Social networks like Facebook can spread moods. BBC News: Study: http://www.bbc.com/news/technology-26556295

11. Orriss, M. (2004). The Karpman Drama Triangle, CSA: http://coachingsupervisionacademy.com/thought-leadersh

Customer Care Guidelines

Chapter Outline

Learning Objectives

After reading this chapter, the reader should be able to:

- Understand the essentials and reasons for customer care
- Recognize the importance of using positive language
- Understand the importance of customer care in various job functions within the airline industry
- Identify and use magic phrases according to different scenarios

BASIC GUIDELINES

Customer satisfaction is not difficult to achieve, but frontline service staff must offer service in the right way. Saying something or doing something at an inappropriate time or place can frustrate customers. It is important for frontline staff to always keep the golden rule of treating others how one wants to be treated in mind.

Facial expression
Keep smiling

> A smile alone doesn't guarantee excellent customer service, but excellent customer service almost always starts with a smile.
>
> Kaan Turnali[1]

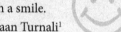

A smile is an international universal gesture of welcomeness, and all great customer service begins and ends with a smile. Apart from indicating the willingness and happiness of the service agent to serve, a simple smile can also convey the following:

- Builds relationship
  - Ready to offer assistance
  - Demonstrate confidence and ability to solve problems
  - Makes customers feel worthy
- Eases uncertainties
  - Diminishes customers' worries
  - Influences the customers' emotions and pacifies them

A smile is not limited to only face-to-face interactions. Customers can also sense a service agent's smile through telephone conversations.

Acknowledge the customer
As soon as a customer approaches, service agents should seek to offer their assistance immediately. If this not possible, they can make eye contact with customers who are waiting. An acknowledgement smile demonstrates that

the agent is aware that a customer is waiting and assures the latter that they will be with them as soon as the transaction with another customer or personnel is finished.

Eye contact

Eye contact is a powerful communication tool. Making eye contact with customers demonstrates attentiveness and shows that service agents respect, are focused on and show interest in what the customers have to say.

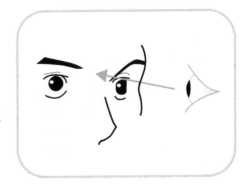

Figure 4-1: Look between the eyes to maintain eye contact.

For those who are not comfortable making eye contact with strangers, this can be overcome with practice. Directing one's gaze between one's eyes can also help to create the effect of maintaining eye contact.

Communication techniques
Listen before responding

Service agents may need to attend to various customers' requests multiple times a day. Over time, they may be accustomed to giving a standard response or one that is based on a similar question or request that they have encountered previously. Service agents should refrain from doing so as they will then be making an assumption without a clear and thorough understanding of what a customer wants.

Service agents should also adopt the practice of allowing customers to finish their questions or sentences before giving any comment or response.

Honesty

It is essential for frontline staff to tell the truth at all times. Hiding information or telling lies can damage the trust and relationship that customers have with airline companies. Frontline staff may get away temporarily without telling customers the complete truth. However, if customers find out about it at a later time, there may be repercussions. In fact, their level of dissatisfaction with the airline can be even higher if they had noticed a problem earlier and conveyed the same to frontline staff. Two common "lies" listed by customers are failure to keep promises and offering false information.

> During check in, Mr. Simon was informed that his connecting flight was delayed due to severe weather conditions. While waiting at the boarding gate for this flight, he went online and found out that the aircraft was delayed due to some passengers who were late for the first leg of the flight. He became angry and called the airline hotline to file a formal complaint about the misleading information given by the service agent.

Enthusiasm

It is important for airline staff to show enthusiasm in their conversations. Even though the same message is repeated many times throughout the day, passengers will only hear it once. A tired and bored tone of voice will affect passengers' reception to the message, in turn affecting the professionalism of an airline. As such, service agents should strive to maintain their enthusiasm at all times.

Failure to keep promises

Instead of resolving customers' problems on the spot, some frontline staff may need to attend to other urgent matters and direct these customers to other colleagues. There are also times when a service agent is unable to sort out customers' problems within a short time frame, hence prolonging the waiting time. While this may be unavoidable in certain situations, it is important to ensure that a service agent is assigned to follow up on customers' query or request. Failure to do so will result in a higher level of customer dissatisfaction and give the impression that the airline is not attentive to its customers.

Mr. Gerald requested for an upgrade from economy class to business using the air miles he had accumulated in his account. However, when the check-in agent tried to process his request, the system was temporarily down. The check-in agent then asked Mr. Gerald to return approximately 20 minutes later as she had to call the frequent-flier center. However, when he returned half an hour later, it seemed that the agent had totally forgotten about his request and he lodged a complaint.

A customer activated the flight attendant call button and asked for a cup of ice water. A cabin crew acknowledged his request but continued distributing headphones to the other passengers. The customer activated the call button again 15 minutes later and became very angry as the cabin crew had forgotten about his request.

Offer adequate information

Providing inadequate information is akin to lying as it results in customers feeling that service agents are dishonest. Integrity plays an important role in developing trust between an airline company and its customers. If the customers find out that an airline does not provide reliable information, a feeling of disappointment and distrust is generated. As such, when accurate information is not available, it is better for service agents to ask customers to check back at a later time when the more details are available instead of relaying half truths.

The most common instances of false information being disseminated are pertaining to seating arrangement and irregular operations.

Seating problems often occur during full flights when customers are unable to get their desired seats. For example, a customer who is assigned to a middle seat may request to have an aisle or window seat instead. If the service agent is already aware that it is impossible to have the seat changed, they should inform the customer right away rather than asking him or her to check again at a later time.

While it may seem nice to give customers a glimmer of hope in the above-mentioned scenario, they will feel even more disappointed when their requests are declined later. This will also minimize any potential conflicts and discrepancies.

In times of irregular operations such as flight delays and cancellations, it is important for airlines to disclose accurate information to passengers. By providing a detailed explanation in order for passengers to understand the situation, further arrangements can then be made to rectify the situation. Refrain from providing inaccurate information as nowadays, customers can easily find out the truth from online.

> An agent told a customer that the flight is delayed due to late incoming aircraft and that aircraft cannot depart from the other airport due to bad weather conditions. However, the customer found out online that the aircraft was due to mechanical problems. The customer was very upset as the service agent did not tell him the truth and lied as to avoid giving out amenities due to the delay. This resulted in the customer losing trust in the airline as well as the image of the airline being damaged.

Talking behind customers' back

It is unprofessional for service agents to talk behind someone else's back, be it whether they are internal or external customers.

At the customer contact center, service agents must ensure that they have either successfully put the customers on hold or completely hung up the line before moving on to another task.

Passengers who travel together do not always check in or board their flights at the same time. If a service agent talks bad about a particular customer, there is a chance that their friends or family may overhear the conversation.

Cabin crew and service agents should also refrain from talking about a customer in the galley area as there is still a chance that the customer may walk pass and overheard what the cabin crew are saying.

In addition, service agents should never assume customers speak a particular language based on their appearance as they may understand and speak multiple languages.

According to Tim Gould, editor of *HR Morning*, the leading source for human resource and employment law news and analysis, a manager

Figure 4-2: Talking behind a customer's back is unprofessional.

has the responsibility of convey the following message to service agents who have spoken ill about customers behind their backs, "It's not helpful the way you talk about our customers behind their backs. It poisons the attitude of the others in customer service. From now on, if you can't say something supportive of a customer, please don't say anything at all." Instead of bearing the risk of having customers hear about the discussion, it is best to refrain from speaking bad about them.[2]

Knowledgeable

Being knowledgeable helps one to build an element of trust with customers. When service agents understand what customers need, they are able to address the root of the problem. Knowledgeable service agents also demonstrate that they care about their guests as they are well prepared for their duties.

Unknowledgeable Staff	Knowledgeable Staff
The cabin crew does not know the answer and needs to check with other cabin crew.	The cabin crew recalled the purser mentioned during the briefing session earlier that pork with noodle and chicken with rice will be served.
Dialogue: I am sorry, sir. I am not sure. Please give me a moment. I'll find out and get back to you.	Dialogue: For today's lunch, the meal options are pork with noodle and chicken with rice. We will also be serving in-flight meals in approximately 20 minutes.

Example

A customer seated in economy class asks a cabin crew about the in-flight lunch options available soon after takeoff.

Response techniques

Responding to customers' request requires some techniques and these are essential skills that all service agents need to acquire as customers will perceive their responses differently. Even if agents are fully aware that a customer's requests cannot be fulfilled, they should check again to be sure instead of replying immediately as a negative prompt reply may create a negative impression that the agent is not helpful.

For example, when an agent declines a customer's request for an aisle seat immediately without even checking, this shows that the agent is not attentive. As such, even if service agents are aware that the flight is completely full and there is no vacant seat available, they need to check the system again so as to give customers the impression that they have done their best to assist them.

Reply with apologies

Apologizing to a customer does not necessarily mean that a service agent has made a mistake or done something wrong. Sometimes it can be because the service agent is unable to offer what the customer wants and in the instance, an apology can be used to convey, politeness and regrets.

Providing alternatives

At times when a service agent is unable to fulfill customers' request, he or she can provide other options for them to choose from. By giving alternative options, customers will feel that they have some control over the situation.

Providing recommendations

In instances whereby the proposed alternative is not the best choice available, service agents may choose to provide other recommendations or opinions by informing customers that what they already have on hand is the best option. This demonstrates that service agents are helpful and care about them. However, it is up to the customers to decide if they would like to take up said advice or recommendation.

"Sorry" vs. "Apologies"

Saying "sorry" and apologizing doesn't necessarily mean the same thing. In fact, apologies are much more formal as opposed to saying "sorry". In addition, the former is used in professional terms and shows less emotions while the latter has a stronger personal touch.

Saying "sorry" or apologizing also conveys different meanings in various contexts. In the airline industry, these words are used in different situations. Apologies are often used when service agents need to deliver bad news to customers and as these service agents represent the company, it is important to maintain professionalism. Below is an example:

"My apologies, sir. Today's flight is full and we are unable to change your seat."

On the other hand, the word "sorry" conveys personal feelings. When service agents have made a mistake, they usually use the word "sorry". Below is an example:

"I am sorry, sir. I'll get a towel to clean up the spillage."

Apologize only when necessary

While it is polite to say "sorry" or apologize, service agents should only do so when necessary as it may potentially cause situations in which customers could transfer the blame to service agents. In instances when the problem is caused by the customers, it is not necessary to apologize. However, service agents can show care and concern via other ways. Below is an example: *A customer spilled orange juice over himself.*

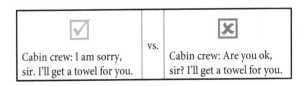

☑	vs.	☒
Cabin crew: I am sorry, sir. I'll get a towel for you.		Cabin crew: Are you ok, sir? I'll get a towel for you.

Surprises

Service agents play an important role in fostering closer bonds between an airline and its customers. This can be done by creating unexpected surprises and memorable flight experiences. Below is a verbatim from a passenger based on a pleasant flight experience after a service agent found out that another passenger was traveling on his birthday upon checking his travel documents, and immediately informed the cabin crew.

"The flight attendant came on near the end of flight, called [the] passenger out by name asked him to ring his call bell. He did and the flight attendant explained that they knew it was his birthday. She then asked all of us to turn on our call buttons, lighting them up as candles and asked [that] we all sing 'Happy Birthday'. After we did, we all turned off our call buttons to 'blow out' the candles. They then delivered a bottle of champagne to the guy. Nice touch."[3]

Westjet Gives a Christmas Surprise to Travelers[4]
Published on December 9, 2013 | Flight Centre Staff
    Article reprinted with permission from Flight Centre.
    Airports are sometimes the least of jolly places to spend your holidays with some travelers facing delays, cancellations or other mishaps. But our friends at WestJet decided to treat travelers to a Christmas miracle by having 150 WestJet employees take on the role as Santa's Little Helpers.
    The airline set up a station with a virtual Santa at Toronto Pearson Airport and Hamilton International Airport for travelers waiting to board their flights to Calgary. Once they told Santa what they wanted for Christmas, the Westjet team took off on shopping sprees to find those items so people could receive their Christmas wishlist upon landing in Calgary.
 To find out more, watch the video below:
    https://www.youtube.com/watch?v=zIEIvi2MuEk

From audio to visual

Visual forms of communication is often more powerful as compared to verbal communication and can even help overcome communication barriers. According to research conducted by the University of Minnesota, School of Management, visual aids are effective communication tools and people tend to recall information much more easily when visual support is available as opposed to mere listening.[5] Hence, using a combination of both verbal and visual communication allows the message to be transmitted and processed successfully.

At times, it may be difficult to explain to customers about their assigned seats. While service agents are familiar with the aircraft's seat map, this may not be the same for passengers, especially for those who do not travel often. Therefore, offering visual information will help service agents to better inform customers about their seating arrangements.

Customers: Where exactly are our seats located?

Service agent: Mr. and Mrs. Jeffery, your assigned seats are on the third row of the economy cabin, on the right. Based on the system, both of you will be seated together and Mrs. Jeffery will be having the window seat.

Customers: I'm sorry. I don't quite understand what you're saying.

Service agent: No worries. I'll explain it in details. The configuration of the aircraft is 3-3 and you have been allocated seats on the right side of the plane. Both of you will be seated together— Mrs. Jeffery will be having the window seat and Mr. Jeffery is assigned to a middle seat. Here is a map with the seats indicated. This will give you a clearer idea of the location of your seats.

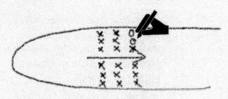

Positive language

When talking to customers or responding to their requests, service agents should always choose the right words to avoid offending customers. While all customers expect their requests to be met, this is not always possible. However, the use of positive language can make a lot of difference when handling such situations.

Negative language

The use of negative language often creates a favorable impression and can potentially damage the relationship between service agents and customers. The following list of negative language may result in customers having a bad impression of an airline and its service staff.

No.	Wait.	I am busy right now.	I cannot help you.
Hang on.	What's your problem?	That does not concern my department. You'll have to speak with someone else.	I don't know.
Calm down.	I can't do that.	I'll have to call you back later.	Listen!

Some customers who are more sensitive may even interpret such responses as service agents not being willing to help or even being rude. As such, refraining from using negative language will minimize misunderstandings from occurring.

Phrase	Explanation
You must ... **You should ...**	Customers may feel that the service agents are giving them orders or instructions and may feel uncomfortable being directed after paying for services.
As I have told you ...	This implies that customers have not been listening or paying attention during the conversation and that service agents need to repeat a message. This will create the impression that agents are blaming the customers.
To be honest ...	From the customers' point of view, this simply means that what was communicated in the previous conversation is untrue and service agents may end up losing credibility.

(Continued)

Phrase	Explanation
Your claim that ... **You told me that ...** **You've stated that ...**	These mean that service agents do not believe what the customer has said and suggest that the customer is lying.
I might be able to ...	This demonstrates that service agents either do not have the confidence or are not able to do something.
I think ...	This shows that service agents are not familiar with their jobs.
Impossible ...	This indicates that service agents do not believe the customers or even imply that they are lying.
This is not within my job scope.	Even though this may be true, the customers do not know the different service agents' job scope and responsibilities. Replying to a request or demand in such a manner may imply these service agents are not willing to offer assistance.
It's not a big deal.	It demonstrates that the customer is a creating a hoo-ha and that the issue raised is a minor problem and that here is no cause for concern. Service agents should always endeavor to treat all problems equally and seek to resolve them in the shortest time possible.
Don't tell anyone I said this ...	This demonstrates unprofessionalism as customers may have the impression that service agents are gossiping about something or someone. While using such phrases to give the impression of confiding in someone may help to create a positive relation between service agents and individual customers, it only serves to damage the overall company's relationship with customers.
The policy stated that ...	This shows that the service agents are strictly following the book and do not show any flexibility and willingness to help customers.
I've never heard anyone complain about this.	Most customers simply choose not to engage an airline's service again after encountering an unpleasant experience and walk away without lodging a complaint as it is time consuming for them to escalate an issue to the airline. A negative response like this implies that customers are creating problems for the airline. Service agents always should treat each complaint seriously.
Compensation	Some customers may have the impression that whenever an airline offers some form of compensation, it must be the airline's fault. However, there are many other unprecedented situations that are beyond an airline's control. In such cases, the phrase "gesture of goodwill" can be used instead.

Below are some scenarios whereby negative and positive phrases are used:

Scenario	Negative response	What it means to customers	Suggested positive response
A customer approached the counter.	Yes?	The service agent acknowledges the customer in a rude manner.	Can I help you?
Can I sit next to the window?	No, the flight is full.	The service agent replies immediately and without offering an alternative solution. This gives the impression that the service agent is unhelpful.	I am not sure, but I'll check. My apologies. The flight is already full and all the other passengers have already checked in.
A customer does not have a valid visa to enter a country.	You must get a visa in order to enter USA.	This gives the impression of directing customers.	A visa is required for entering USA.
The customer informed a service agent that he was told by another agent that he is allowed to check in 50 kg of baggage without additional charges.	Impossible!	Nothing is impossible as long as efforts are made to get things done. This conveys impoliteness and unprofessionalism.	My apologies. I cannot comment on this as I was not at the scene when the prior conversation took place. I will check and see what I can do about this.
A customer complained about a previous flight delay experience while checking in.	Really?	The service agent does not believe what the customer is saying.	Thank you for sharing this experience with us.
A handicapped customer asked for a wheelchair.	I might be able to organize that for you.	This shows that service agents are not familiar with their job scope.	Sure. I will make the necessary arrangements.
A customer asked a service agent about the boarding time.	I think we can start boarding in approximately 10 minutes.	This shows that service agents are not familiar with their job scope.	Boarding will begin in 10 minutes.
A customer is complained about being unable to reserve a window seat.	It's not a big deal.	The customer may be offended that service agents do not take their complaints seriously.	My apologies, I will see what I can do.

(Continued)

Scenario	Negative response	What it means to customers	Suggested positive response
A customer approached the service counter and asked for a free upgrade to business class.	**To be honest**, I do not have the authority to do so.	The customer may feel that the service agent is not telling the truth.	My apologies, courtesy upgrade is not available for this flight.
A customer was late for check in and demanded a boarding pass.	**We can't** do that.	Service agents should not turn customers away without offering any help or solutions.	I am sorry, sir. It is already past the check-in time for this flight. I will see what I can do to help you.
A customer complained about an airline's service.	Many customers have similar complaints. By the way, **don't tell anyone I've said this.**	This demonstrates that service agents are not satisfied with their own company. It will damage the trust and relationship between an airline and its customers.	Thank you for your comments and feedback. We will look into this matter.
A customer requested for an additional blanket after an initial request was declined.	**As I have told you**, we have run out of blankets.	Avoid using the phrase "As I have told you …" as it conveys curtness.	My apologies, sir. We have run out of blankets.
A customer who has had too much alcoholic beverages on board the flight requested for more wine.	**We cannot** give you more.	This is unprofessional and conveys curtness.	I am sorry, sir. I am afraid that we will not be able to offer you any more alcoholic drinks. Would you like some water instead?
A customer asked a senior cabin crew staff for assistance to store a hand-carry baggage in the overhead bin.	**This is not my duty.**	This shows that the cabin staff is rude and not willing to help.	Sure. Let's lift it together.
A customer wanted to buy duty free items on-board a flight. The airline only accepts credit card but the customer wanted to pay in cash.	Due to the **company's policy**, we only accept credit cards. I am sorry but there's nothing I can do.	This reflects that the cabin staff is not accommodating and simply follows the book.	My apologies, madam. We can only accept credit cards. Perhaps you can ask your friend or family member who is traveling with you if they have a credit card.

(Continued)

Scenario	Negative response	What it means to customers	Suggested positive response
A customer requested for chicken rice during the meal service. However, there is none left.	We **don't have** any chicken rice left. Do you want pork noodles?	The cabin staff is pushing customers into making a choice.	My apologies, sir. Unfortunately, we are out of chicken rice. Would you like to have some pork noodles instead?
A customer asked for Coca Cola Zero.	I am sorry, we **don't have** this.	The cabin crew does not offer an alternative.	I am sorry, we do not serve coke on this flight. Can I bring you a can of Diet Pepsi instead?
The customer complained about the quality of the in-flight meals.	I **have never heard anyone complain about this.**	This may suggest that the customer is a trouble maker when he/she may be trying to give some constructive feedback.	Thank you for your comments and feedback. We will look into this matter.
The customer complained about a flight diversion due to a sick passenger who had to be transported to the hospital immediately.	We will offer you a **compensation** of USD200 worth of travel vouchers.	The sick customer required immediate medical attention. As such, it is not the airline's fault for the flight delay.	We apologize for the delay. As a gesture of goodwill, we will offer you USD200 worth of travel vouchers.

Negative gestures

Body languages often convey various meanings. As such, service agents must avoid demonstrating negative gestures as they may be interpreted differently by customers and miscommunications can be sometimes created, which will in turn affect the airline's reputation.

In such instances, service agents may choose to use verbal communication when communicating with certain customers. Service agents can then carefully choose their choice of words to ensure effective communication.

The magic phrases

Entrepreneur Media, a leading publisher that delivers content about independent thinkers, builders, and leaders driving economies has suggested several magic phrases that can be used for effective communication.[6]

1. "How can I help you?"

This allows customers to start a conversation with service agents.

Scenarios	
An anxious looking customer approaches the check-in counter. The customer service agent asks "How can I help you?" and the customer replies "I've lost my passport."	A customer pushes the service bell. The cabin crew approaches the customer and asks "How can I help you?" The customer replies "I want to change my seat. I don't want to sit next to the lavatory."

2. "I can assist you with your problem."

Customers are always relieved to know that there is someone to attend to them and solve their problems.

Scenarios	
The customer service agent says "I can assist you with this problem. Do you have your driver license?" The customer replies "Yes". The service agent then answers "This is a domestic flight and you may use your driver license as your identification document."	The cabin crew replies "I can assist with this problem. We have several seats available in the rear cabin. Would you like to shift to that seat instead?"

3. "I am not sure, but I'll find out."

In instances whereby service agents are unable to answer customers' questions immediately, this phrase can be used to buy some time. Some customers may also challenge service agents with questions that are not within their capacity to answer. This sentence allows service agents to contact the someone who is in the best position to answer said question.

Scenarios	
The customer asked "How long does it need to get a passport replacement?" The service agent replied "I am not sure, but I'll found out."	The customer asked "How about business class? Are there any seats available?" The cabin crew replied "I am not sure, but I'll find out."

4. "I will keep you updated."

When service agents are unable to give an immediate response, this sentence can be used to inform customers about the status of their request once more information is available.

Scenarios	
An announcement about a flight delay was made at the boarding gate and the customer approached the service agent "What is the departure time?" The service agent replied "The exact departure time is not yet available. I will keep you updated via the public announcement system."	The in-flight entertainment system is not working properly and the purser tried to reset it. A customer activated the service bell and asked "When can I continue watching my movie?" The cabin crew replied "We are still fixing the system. I will keep you updated."

5. "I appreciate your business."

This is used to thank customers for their patience while waiting for service agents to assist them or resolve their problems.

Scenarios	
A previously delayed flight is now ready for boarding, and service agents approach customers "We apologize for the delay. Boarding will commence in 5 minutes. We appreciate your business."	During disembarkation, the purser thanks every passenger in the business class cabin "Thank you for flying with us. We appreciate your business."

6. "Thank you"

This can be used to show appreciation in any situation. It is also useful to end a conversation or service transaction by thanking the customers.

Scenarios	
After informing customers about a flight delay, the service agent added "My apologies for the flight delay and thank you for your understanding."	After a service agent has checked a customer's boarding pass, she says "We wish you a pleasant flight. Thank you for flying with us."

Customer care over the phone

Service agents must pay extra attention when handling customers over the phone as the message is delivered verbally over the telephone line.

Background noise

While communicating with customers over the phone, service agent must be aware of any potention background noise in their surrounding environment as customers can easily pick up them up. These background noises often create the impression that the service agents do not care about their customers as they affect the quality of the calls. Below are some points to note:

- Noise from other service agents can be easily heard by customers. Background laughter will convey the impression that staff are not serious in handling their jobs.
- Agents should never eat or drink while on a call as this affects the clarity of the conversation. In addition, it is unprofessional to chew and swallow food and drinks while speaking to customers.
- Service agents should also avoid breathing heavily into the speaker or microphone. It creates unpleasant breathing noises which is magnified on the other end of the call.

Avoiding putting customers on hold

Service agents working at the customer care center may sometimes be required to put customers on hold so as to retrieve more information, consult with other colleagues or look into alternative solutions to resolve customers' problems. Before placing customers on hold, agents should ask for their contacts in the event that the line gets disconnected.

Whenever possible, agents should also avoid placing angry customers on hold as they are already dissatisfied with an issue, and there is a chance that some of them have already waited a long time to get through the line. Placing these customers on hold will create further negativity. Moreover, customers will feel that service agents are not knowledgeable and are not being helpful.

Service agent: Mr. Saxon, can you please hold on while I retrieve your reservation?

Customer: Ok.

Service agent: Thank you for waiting, Mr. Saxon. I am afraid that I will need to put you on hold again as I have to call the airport to reconfirm your seat assignment. Can I please have your contact just in case the line gets disconnected?

Customer: Sure. 9874-3895

Service agent: Thank you.

Service agent: Thank you for waiting, Mr. Saxon. I have contacted our airport staff and your seat has been confirmed. It is 34A; a window seat. The check-in counters will be open 3 hours before departure and the counter is located at Terminal A. Is there anything else I can help you with?

Customer: That's fantastic. No, that's all for now. Thank you for your help.

Waiting time

Service agents should always let customers know the purpose of having to put them on hold, as that they will better understand the situation. Whenever possible, service agents should also let customers know about the approximate waiting time.

Service agent: I am sorry. Mrs. Chen. Can I put you on hold for two minutes while I change your reservation?

There are other instances whereby waiting cannot be avoided due to operational reasons, and flights and services have to be delayed to ensure the safety of all passengers. In such cases, the service agent should always keep customers up to date on information related to the flight status, approximate waiting time and reasons for the delay.

Service agent: Mrs. Janet, can you please hold while I retrieve your reservation?

Customer: Sure.

Service agent: Thank you for waiting, Mrs. Janet. I have made the changes to the flight reservation as per your requests.

Customer: Thank you.

Service agent: You are welcome. Is there anything else I can help you with?

Customer: No, thank you.

In instances when the aircraft is flying through turbulence, pilots may need to make an announcement to inform cabin crew and passengers that all services will be terminated temporarily. This announcement serves to inform customers that they will need to wait for some time before services are resumed.

Cabin crew, please return to your station. Ladies and gentlemen, the aircraft is now flying through areas of turbulence, please return to your seat and fasten your seat belts. All services will now be suspended and will resume once we are out of the turbulence area. We apologize for any inconvenience caused.

Handling large groups of travelers

Customers may sometimes be accompanied by their family and friends while checking in. There may be instances whereby they may make requests on behalf of the passenger and might even be upset when the demands cannot be fulfilled.

Attend to the customers directly

It is a good practice to communicate and explain all necessary flight information to the passenger. At the same time, service agents should try to answer all valid and reasonable questions and demands.

Identify the leader

When customers are traveling in a group, it is more effective to communicate with the leader of the group such as the tour guide or an individual who serves as the representative. The leader can then convey the messages to the other passengers. This is especially helpful when the members in a tour group are foreigners and the tour leader is the middleman. The tour leader is also the key person who helps to eliminate any potential barriers of communication.

Special needs customers

Service agents must be extra cautious and attentive when attending to passengers with special needs, such as the physically disabled and those with mental impairment. There are times whereby showing too much care and concern can be annoying even when service agents mean well as both overcaring and lack of care can sometimes be considered as a form of discrimination. The best approach in such cases is to check with the customers directly to find out whether they need assistance before asking them what is the best way to offer help.

Assistance to the gate?

A service agent noticed a customer was on a wheelchair. She approached him and asked if he needed assistance in making his way to the boarding gate. The passenger refused politely and said that he could manage it. As the customer was about to leave the check-in counter, another agent approached the customer and he once again, declined the offer of help. Shortly after, a third agent tried to offer assistance and at this point, the customer became very annoyed. He retorted "I have been on the wheelchair for 10 years and I know how to manage this myself. I am only physically disabled and I am not stupid. I will ask for help if I need it!"

Fairness for all
Be consistent

All customers expect to be treated equally, and some basic and standardized services such as helpful staff and high standards of safety regulation should be made available to all customers regardless of cabin class. However, service agents should never compromise an airline's policies simply to please customers as this would result in inconsistent services. Below is a verbatim from a disgruntled passenger who has been on the receiving end of inconsistent customer service:

"Your airline staff in Singapore are more helpful than the ones in this airport as they allowed me to check in an extra bag for free. Why you are giving me trouble today and asking me to pay?"

A customer was allowed to check in an extra piece of baggage for free on a previous flight. On a separate trip month later, the customer decided to travel with the same airline as he was very satisfied with his prior experience. He also expected that the agents will be lenient with the baggage allowance. However, the service agent who was serving him complied with the airline's policies and he had to pay for the excess baggage.

Sense of humor

On some occasions, joking with customers can increase customers' satisfaction level or even diffuse a tense situation. However, not all customers have the same sense of humor and therefore, service agents need to make their best judgments after observing a customer's personality and act according to the situation.

Customer:	It is a long flight. Can you assign a pretty lady to sit next to me?
Service agent:	Yes, of course. One of our staff is the winner of Miss Universe 1940. Would you like her to sit next to you?
Customer:	Ha ha. Yes, please!

Other customer care techniques
Attitude

Attitude is subjective. When a customer is not satisfied with a particular staff, they may sometimes lodge a complaint on the basis that a staff has an attitude problem. As such, it is essential for service agents to be able to decline a customer's request in a tactful manner, without the customer becoming offended.

Offering compensation

When the airline offers compensation, customers may assume that the airline has made mistakes and compensation is offered as a gesture of apology. However, there are some occasions which an airline is not at fault but the company continues to offer benefits so as to maintain a good relationship with customers. In such cases, a "gesture of goodwill" is used. This means that the airline does not admit to any liability, but on the other hand, it offers customers a good or service in order to retain their loyalty.

Figure 4-3: Do not eat in front of the customers at all times.

> Mr. Genting's in-flight entertainment system malfunctioned during a flight from Singapore to Tokyo and he was unable to finish watching his movie. As a "gesture of goodwill", he received food vouchers and an upgrade to a lay-flat seat. This shows that the airline values the long-term relationship with its customers.

No eating and drinking

Consumption of food and drinks in front of customers is strictly forbidden as it is demonstrates unprofessionalism. Doing so sends the message that service agents do not care about their duties.

Don't take things personally

Some customers may get irritated due to various reasons but service agents should not take it personally as the majority of customers' grievances is due to dissatisfaction with an airline's policy or operation. The role that service agents need to play in such instances is to handle customers in a professional manner and keep calm at all times.

Figure 4-4: Do not eat when handling phone calls.

Learn from mistakes

No one is perfect and we all make mistakes. Service agents need to admit they are wrong and make sure to not repeat the same mistake. Customers are usually more tolerant towards new staff and some airlines required these staff to wear a different uniform or put on a badge to indicate that they are trainees.

> ## Mistake
>
> Well, we all make mistakes, dear, so just put it behind you. We should regret our mistakes and learn from them, but never carry them forward into the future with us.
>
> **L.M. Montgomery, Anne of Avonlea**[7]

Safety as a priority

While safety and services are some basic expectations of customers, safety is an airline's first priority and it overwrites all aspects of customer service. In other words, airline service agents may choose to suspend services when a safety issue arises. Any issues related to safety must be handled with top priority, and no flexibility nor alternative options will be offered to customers. Below are some examples:

- A customer wanted to check-in his baggage containing radioactive materials. His request was declined by the service agent.
- A pregnant customer was refused a seat in the exit row, as she is not fit enough to performing the evacuation duties of an exit row passenger.
- All in-flight services are suspended when an aircraft is flying through areas with severe turbulence and passengers are strictly not allowed to use the restrooms.

SUMMARY

Excellent customer care comprises various techniques. These include facial expressions, excellent communication skills and response skills. On occasions whereby verbal communication cannot successfully deliver a message, visual aid may be used. In addition, it is important for service agents to use positive language during conversations to demonstrate politeness and helpfulness. While there is no single formula in achieving excellent customer service, service agents must pay attention to their attitude at all times and be flexible enough when dealing with customers' complaints and requests, without going against the airline's rules and regulations.

Airline a Great Support during a Stressful Time[8]
—By Sherry Graves-Morrison and Bill Morrison (Russell, Ont.)
Article reprinted with permission from Winnipeg Free Press

OUR Canadian airlines are always getting such bad press. I want to tell you all about the fabulous treatment my husband and I received recently from WestJet Airlines.

While on a personal weekend trip to Winnipeg from Ottawa, my husband took ill but managed to get to the airport by 8 a.m. in time for the 9 o'clock direct flight home to Ottawa.

The WestJet personnel were concerned he did not look well, and they called [the] paramedics. They administered oxygen and transported him to the emergency department at Grace Hospital.

At this stage, Paula—WestJet's guest services manager, employee No. 6164—became my liaison. She contacted me at work in Ottawa and let me know the situation.

A WestJet employee [even] went to the hospital and stayed with my husband, relaying any update on his condition.

Every hour or so, Paula would call me with an update. She kept me more informed than I could have done on my own. She advised [that] WestJet would arrange to fly me to Winnipeg at any time if I decided I should join my husband there.

On her urging, I made arrangements to travel to Winnipeg on the next direct flight, and Paula made sure all my needs were taken care of. She gave me her work schedule and the name and direct phone number of her replacement.

Tyler, employee No. 9307, met me at the arrival gate and was equally concerned and supportive. He presented me with taxi chits for travel to and from the hospital and the hotel where a room was booked, and picked up and stored my luggage until we determined whether my husband was able to fly back home that day or if we were staying overnight. As the morning flight was direct and would be much faster, we stayed overnight, and my bag was delivered to the hotel.

Tyler met us at the airport the next morning, got us priority boarding and ensured wheelchair assistance was arranged in Winnipeg and at our destination in Ottawa.

At every stage, during such a stressful time created by an unforeseen medical situation, WestJet staff were 100 per cent supportive.

What a wonderful company! WestJet obviously empowers its staff to be able to act to suit each situation and really knows the meaning of customer service and support.

APPLYING THE KNOWLEDGE

Look at the pictures and answer the questions.

	This gesture means: _____ What does it demonstrate? _____ _____ _____ _____ _____
	This gesture means: _____ What does it demonstrate? _____ _____ _____ _____ _____
	This gesture means: _____ What does it demonstrate? _____ _____ _____ _____ _____
	This gesture means: _____ What does it demonstrate? _____ _____ _____ _____ _____

This gesture means: _____

What does it demonstrate?

_____
_____
_____
_____
_____

This gesture means: _____

What does it demonstrate?

_____
_____
_____
_____
_____

This gesture means: _____

What does it demonstrate?

_____
_____
_____
_____
_____

This gesture means: _____

What does it demonstrate?

_____
_____
_____
_____
_____

This gesture means: _____

What does it demonstrate?

_____
_____
_____
_____

This gesture means: _____

What does it demonstrate?

_____
_____
_____
_____
_____

ENDNOTES

1. Turnali, K. (2004, Dec 14) .4 Reasons Why Excellent Customer Service Should Start With A Smile. Forbes:http://www.forbes.com/sites/sap/2014/12/14/4-reasons-why-excellent-customer-service-should-start-with-a-smile/

2. Gould, T. (2015, Mar 25). Dealing with acidic attitudes: Help for your managers.HRmorning.com: http://www.hrmorning.com/managers-dealing-with-negative-attitudes/

3. Phelps, S. (2014). Southwest Airlines does a creative little extra for a passenger.9 inch marketing: http://www.9inchmarketing.com/2014/03/23/southwest-airlines-does-a-creative-little-extra-for-a-passenger/

4. Flight Centre Staff. (2013, Dec 9). Westjet Gives a Christmas Surprise to Travellers. Travel Blog: http://www.flightcentre.ca/blog/westjet-gives-christmas-surprise-travellers/

5. Hanke, J. (1998). The Psychology of Presentation Visuals, www.presentations.com

6. Annoyomous. (2013, Mar 14). The 10 Magic Phrases of Customer Service. Enterpreneur: http://www.entrepreneur.com/article/226062

7. Montgomery, L. M. (1909). Anne of Avolea. Xist Publishing. CA.

8. Graves, S. (2015). Airline a great support during a stressful time. Winnipeg free press: http://www.winnipegfreepress.com/opinion/blogs/kindness/Airline-a-great-support-during-a-stressful-time-318445081.html#comments

CHAPTER FIVE

Airline Customer Service Policies

Chapter Outline

Learning Objectives

After reading this chapter, the reader should be able to:

- Recognize customer service policy
- Identify the different consumer protection policies offered by governments and airline associations
- Understand various policy details and how they protect consumers' rights

AIRLINE CUSTOMER SERVICE POLICY

Governments in many countries require airlines to establish customer service policies that protect consumers' rights and these policies apply to specific flight routes of various airports. Consumer protection laws are a form of government regulation that aims to protect customers' rights and covers most of the issues related to air travels. Airlines must offer transparent information and handle disruptions caused by airline operations, and airline service agents must be well trained to handle customers' issues during irregular operations. Under these policies, airlines need to offer adequate assistance and amenities to customers. Otherwise, customers have the right to file a complaint against the airline companies. Some airline associations have developed similar non-mandatory policies and their member airlines have voluntary committed to these policies, which then become the industry's standard.

Details regarding airline customer service policy vary according to countries. In addition, airlines are subjected to the policies of both the country of embarkation and disembarkation. According to International Air Transport Association (IATA)'s statistics, approximately 60 countries have set up such consumer protection polices[1] and these policies apply to both local and foreign airlines.

International policies adopted in the United States (US), European Union (EU), and the International Air Transport Association (IATA) are mandatory for all airlines operating flights to and from and within the region while the IATA's recommended policy is adopted on a voluntary basis by its airline members.

Customer Service Plan—US

The U.S. Department of Transportation first established the Customer Service Plan in September 1999[2] and it governs all airline operators in the United States of America. Subsequently, the rules applied to other airline flights flying into the country.

The customer service plan includes various topics that protected the rights of customers from using the airline's service. These include fare, delay and cancellations, baggage, refunds and complaints.[3]

All US-based airlines and airlines flying into the United States must comply with the Customer Service Plan and state their actions pertaining to each topic. These actions then must be made available for customers' review.

Protection of Air Passenger—EU 🔹

In 2004, the European Commission (EU) passed regulation No. 261/2004 in 2004 in order to enhance consumer protection policies for passengers flying within and to or from European Union countries.[4] The regulation focuses on consumer benefits and established rules on compensation and assistance to passengers when a customer encounters denied boarding, flight cancellations or extended delays of flights.

IATA Core Principles of Consumer Protection—IATA ✈

✳ MUST KNOW! ♥

The International Air Transport Association (IATA) is an airline association representing 265 airlines or 83% of total air traffic in the world. In 2013, IATA endorsed a suggested set of core principles of consumer protection regulation for the government. Member airlines can also decide whether they would like to subscribe to IATA's Core Principles of Consumer Protection.[5]

In order to comply with policies adopted by the respective airlines, service agents must understand them in details in order to provide customers with accurate information and appropriate assistance.

POLICY DETAILS

The international consumer protections for air travelers are somewhat similar for EU, US and IATA. In addition, the customer policy regulated by policy makers can be divided into the four main components: before travel, during travel, after travel and compensation. The policy states both customers' right and airlines' procedures. The policy also states the responsibilities of airlines and the amenities or compensation offered to affected customers for different scenarios.

1) Before flight
→ Inform passengers about the identity of the carrier (🔲,🔳) INT

The airline must be disclosed to customers when making reservations.
This includes the air carrier or carriers that are or are likely to act as
an operating air carrier, especially in instances of airlines that have a
code-sharing agreement, which may cause confusion as customers may
sometimes be unaware of the airline they are actually flying with.

→ Inform about possible availability of lower fares at direct USA outlets (🔲, 🔳)

Airlines must release information about the lowest available appropriate
fares to customers through various book channels such as call centers,
offices and websites.

In addition, service agents at the airport ticket sales office, reservation
center and website must always offer the lowest fare available based on
customers' requested travel dates.

> **Service agent:** Mr. Lee, the lowest price for the flight date and time that you
> have requested is USD 218, including taxes.

→ Honor the agreed fare after payment (🔳) USA

Airlines are not allowed to increase the airfare after a payment transaction
is completed. This ensures that customers are entitled to the original fare
and package they have paid for.

→ Allow reservations to be held or cancelled (🔳) USA

Airline must allow a reservation to be held at the quoted fare without
payment or cancelled without penalty for a certain period of time after a
reservation is made. This allows customers time to compare fares offered
by other airlines.

Service agent:	Mr. Lee, your reservation is now confirmed. Please note that payment must be paid before 6 pm tomorrow; otherwise the reservation will be automatically cancelled.

Provide prompt ticket refunds (🖳) ← USA

Airlines must commit to a refund within a limited period after the payment is made. The industry standard is 20 days for cash refund and seven days for credit card purchases.

Service agent:	Mr. Lee, your ticket refund has been processed. The amount will be returned to your credit card within the next 7 days.

Waive ticket restrictions (non-refundable, sequential use of flight coupons) in special circumstances (🖳, 📇) ← USA/INT

Airlines can choose to disregard the penalties listed in the customer ticket in special circumstances whereby customers are able to provide proof and evidence of their requests.

Service agent:	Mr. Lee, in order to change your flight as requested, we would like you to send us the supporting documents you have mentioned over the phone. Would you be able to send us these documents either by fax or email?

→ *Ensure pricing transparency (■, ▤)* USA

Prices offered by airlines must list the exact breakdown of the airfare. Additional fees such as taxes, fuel surcharges and convenience fees must be indicated clearly. Airlines must also indicate the exact taxes and fees that make up the cost of the airfare.

→ *Advise passengers on airline commercial and operational conditions (■, ▤, ✈)* USA/INT

Airlines are responsible for informing customers the following:

- flight schedule
- departure and arrival terminal and airport
- number of en-route stop(s) for a flight
- change of aircraft, terminal or airport
- all conditions attached to the total airfare
- operating carrier and corresponding flight number

→ *Protect passengers against carrier insolvency (■)*

Airlines must offer financial compensation to customers in the event of bankruptcy. These can be done via insurance add-ons. As such, airline companies are obliged to offer optional insurance or provide compulsory insurance for their passengers upon booking of air tickets to protect against any potential cases of insolvency.

→ *Inform passengers of future flight disruptions (✈)* INT

Airlines are responsible for informing customers of any flight disruptions and changes whenever such information is made available before the actual date of travel.

→ *Disclose contingency plans, customer service plans and contracts of carriage (carrier website) (▤)* USA

Airlines must disclose their policies for customers' review purposes. Service agents should communicate these policies verbally by service agents at the airline contact center. Written forms of information about these policies must also be made available in the official websites.

Service agent: Mr. Lee, your reservation is confirmed. Please note that this is a promotional ticket, and it is non-refundable and non-changeable.

2) During the flight   USA/INT.
Code-share partners maintain service standards (■, ■, ⬛) ←

Code-sharing is becoming a popular business strategy among airlines. Code-sharing is an agreement made between two different airlines offering services on a single aircraft. Both airlines in a code-sharing agreement must agree with the comparable customer service plan. This ensures that customers receive the same level of customer protection throughout their flight even if they are transferring to other airlines.

Cabin crew: Ladies and gentlemen, welcome to C&M Airline operated with our code sharing partner E&C Airlines. You are now on board flights CM344 and EC 9344, departing from Honolulu to Singapore.

Notify customers of known delays, cancellations and ◀ diversions (■, ⬛)

Delay of flights must be announced to customers in a prompt manner. Many airlines use multiple means of contact to notify customers about irregular operations. These include websites, messages (text messages and emails), calling customers by the airline contact center, and making announcements at the airport terminal either via verbally and visually.

Contact Center

Service agent: Mr. Lee, we regret to inform you that your flight, CM344 from Honolulu to Singapore has been delayed for 2 hours. It has been rescheduled to depart at 1900.

Text: Your flight CM 334 17 Sep 2015 from Honolulu is now changed. The updated scheduled time of departure is now 1900 hr. We apologize for the inconvenience caused.

At the airport: Ladies and gentlemen, may I have your attention please? C&M Airline regrets to inform customers that flight CM344 scheduled to departure Honolulu to Singapore has been delayed due to severe weather conditions. The new expected departure time will be 7 pm. We are sorry for any inconvenience caused.

→ *Provide notification of opportunity to deplane (▤)* USA,

Aircrafts are sometimes unable to take off during lengthy tarmac delays. Airlines should not allow aircrafts to remain on the tarmac for more than three hours, and are obliged to return the aircrafts to the parking area where the customers can disembark from the aircraft and return to the terminal. If the aircraft door is still connected to the jet bridge, the cabin crew should inform customers that they can choose to leave the aircraft during this period.

Cabin crew: Ladies and gentlemen, due to the lengthy delay of this flight, the captain has given approval for all passengers to disembark and return to the passenger terminal. Please retrieve all your personal belongings and get ready for disembarkation. Thank you.

USA/INT.

→ *Assist in case of delay, including long on-aircraft delay (▣, ▤, ﹡)*

During a tarmac delay, airlines should offer customers adequate food and water, no later than 2 hours after the gate departure or touchdown.

In addition, airlines must maintain operable lavatories and, if necessary, provide medical attention to those who may need assistance.[6]

During denied boarding or flight cancellation, airlines are responsible to either offer customers a refund ticket or make arrangements for alternative means of transportation so that customers can continue their journey.

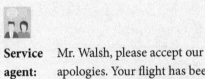

Service agent: Mr. Walsh, please accept our apologies. Your flight has been cancelled. We will arrange for you to travel with our partner airline—A&Z Airline to Rome.

Figure 5-1: Notification of delay.

During an extend delay whereby a flight is delayed for five hours or more, customers are entitled to a full refund of their tickets if they choose not to accept the new flight arrangements provided.

In instances when flights are delayed for more than 2 hours, and customers are being denied boarding or when flights are cancelled, airline service agents must explain the customers' rights to all affected passengers, together with the reasons for irregular operations.

Service agent: Mr. Walsh, please accept our apologies. Your flight has been delayed for 5 hours. We can either arrange for you to travel with our partner, A&Z Airline to Rome or you may also choose to obtain a full refund of your ticket.

In events of extended delays or flight cancellations, airlines must offer amenities to customers. These amenities may include refreshments, meals, free communications or an overnight stay if required. These amenities may vary depending on the flight distance and length of delay.

Service agent: Mr. Walsh. Please accept our apologies. Your flight has been delayed until tomorrow. We would like to offer you one-night stay at the airport's hotel. This stay will include a complimentary dinner and breakfast. The flight will depart tomorrow morning at 10.15 am instead.

→ Handle passenger denied boarding with fairness and consistency (■, ■, ▒) ᴜSᴀ/ Ɪɴᴛ

Overbooking is a common practice in the airline industry, and airlines may not be able to accommodate all customers on a flight due to either over sales or operational reasons. These customers are known as denied boarding customers. In such instances, airlines should first ask for customers to voluntarily give up their seats in exchange for other forms of compensation. However, there are not enough volunteer customers, airlines will then involuntary deny boarding customer(s) according to their check-in time, travel class, frequent flyer status, and/or ease of re-accommodation. Airlines will also need to offer compensation and/or make alternative transportation arrangements for the affected customers.

Service agent: Mr. Lee, our flight is overbooked today. Do you need to travel to Singapore urgently? If not, would you be interested to delay your flight for another two hours in exchange for a USD500 voucher?

→ Delivery baggage on time (■, ■) ᴏSᴀ

Airlines are committed to transport customers' baggage on the aircraft. However, delays may sometimes occur. In such events, airlines should

make every reasonable effort to return any delayed baggage within
24 hours.

At the airport

Service agent: Mr. Lee, we are sorry to inform you that your baggage has
yet to arrive. C&M Airline would like to offer USD70 for
purchase of toiletries. Could you please keep the receipts of
your purchases and contact us for reimbursement?

Properly accommodate disabled customers and those with special needs (■, ▤, ▥) USA/ INT.

The policy requires airlines to offer basic and adequate services to all
customers without any form of discrimination against passengers on
the basis of disabilities. There must be sufficient facilities available at the
airport and facilities inside aircraft cabins must be readily accessed by
and made usable to any customers with disabilities, including those who
require the use of wheelchairs and portable medical electronic devices.

Airlines must also offer assistance to customers who require additional
attention, such as unaccompanied minors and mentally disabled customers
without additional charges.

Cabin crew: Mr. Lee, this aircraft is equipped with an aisle chair. Please
let me know if you need to use the lavatory. I'll have the aisle
chair ready whenever you need it.

---

3) **After the flight**   USA
Submit data for regular consumer report (■, ▤)

Airlines are required to submit a monthly performance report to the
respective authorities, such as the US Department of Transport and the

EU European Commission. Information that need to be included in the report includes flight delay data, mishandled baggage statistics, consumer complaints and other incident reports. The information will then be collected and published by the authorities and made available to the general public.

→ Handling customers' complaints (🇪🇺, 🏅) o Sﾃ/ᴢNT

Airlines must respond to customers' complaints within a stated time period. According to the European Regulation on passengers' rights and US Department of Transport's consumer rule No. 49 U.S.C. §41712, airlines must acknowledge a complaint within 30 days and get in touch with the complainant with a substantive response within 60 days.

4) COMPENSATION

→ Compensation for lost bag (🇪🇺, 🇺🇸) USA

When an airline is unable to retrieve a customer's lost baggage, compensation must be met out.

EU	US
Maximum compensation up to EUR 1,220	Domestic travel: up to USD 3,500 per passenger International travel: up to 1,131 Special Drawing Rights* per passenger.

Special Drawing Rights is a form of currency created by the International Monetary Fund (IMF) for easy conversion of money to both convertible and non-convertible currencies.

→ Compensation for flight cancellation/denied boarding/delay USA (🇪🇺, 🇺🇸)

The EU air passenger rights states the financial compensation that an airline is liable to during ad hoc denied boarding, flight cancellation and delays. Airlines are obliged to offer monetary compensations to customers who are subjected to denied boarding, flight cancellation or arrival at a destination 3 hours later than as stated in the original itinerary.

→ *Delay and cancellation compensation within the EU.*[7]

Delayed time	
2 hours or more	Free meal and refreshments, two free telephone calls, telex or fax messages or emails
5 hours or more	Refund full cost of the ticket
Departure is deferred until the next day	Free meal and refreshment plus two free telephone calls, telex or fax messages, or emails and hotel accommodation

Denied boarding compensation or late arrival of more than 3 hours.[7]

Flight within the EU states	Flight from EU states to non EU countries
1,500 km or less—€250	1,500 km or less—€250
Over 1,500 km—€400	1,500–3,500 km—€400
	Over 3,500 km—€600

→*Delay and cancellation compensation (US)*

There are no official rules for delay and compensation for US carriers. ✵ However, each airline may set up its own compensation policy. The denied boarding compensations are as follows.[8]

No compensation	If the airline offers alternative transportation and the affected passenger arrives at the final destination no later than one hour after the planned arrival time of said passenger's original flight.
Compensation shall be 200% of the fare or a maximum monetary compensation of USD 675	If the airline offers alternative transportation and the affected passenger arrives at the final destination more than one hour but less than two hours after the planned arrival time of said passenger's original flight.
Compensation shall be 400% of the fare or a maximum monetary compensation of USD 1,350	If the airline is unable to offer alternative transportation and the affected passenger arrives at the final destination more than one hour but less than two hours (US airlines) or four hours (foreign airlines) after the planned arrival time of said passenger's original flight.

Other compensation policies

Many countries have also implemented their own consumer protection policies, and are mostly target airlines registered in the respective countries. However, these policies are not as strict as the ones adopted in the Europe and the United States.

Thailand ≡

According to Sections 3 (4), 4, 7 and 9 of the Declaration of the Revolutionary Council No. 58 declared on the 26th of January, B.E. 2515, by the Ministry of Transport, all Thai carrier services on domestic scheduled routes must conform to the Protection of Passenger Rights.[9]

	Flight delay 2–3 hours	Flight delay 3–5 hours	Flight delay 5–6 hours	Flight delay of 6 hours or more/ flight cancellation
Airlines must provide complimentary food and drinks to customers	☑	☑	☑	☑
Offer communication service to customers	☑	☑	☑	☑
Offer full refund to customers if they decide to cancel their trip	☑	☑	☑	☑
Offer alternative flights, alternative destinations close to the original destination or other appropriate travel options	☒	☑	☑	☑
Offer monetary compensation or travel vouchers	☒	☒	THB 600	THB 1,200
Offer accommodation	☒	☒	☒	One night

The People's Republic of China[10] ▓

Hours of delay	Amenities or compensation
1–4 hours	Complimentary food services
4 hours or more	Rest area
4–8 hours	RMB 300 worth of discount or mileage or RMB 200 in cash
8 hours or more	RMB 450 worth of discount or mileage or RMB 300 in cash

India

Monetary compensation is only offered when the fare of the ticket is higher than the compensated amount.[11]

Amount	Conditions
2000 Rupees or the value of the ticket	Delay time of up to and including one hour
3000 Rupees or the value of the ticket	Delay time of more than one hour and up to and including two hours
4000 Rupees or the value of the ticket	Delay time of more than two hours

If the cost of the ticket is less than the amount compensated, airlines are liable to compensate a monetary amount equivalent to the full cost of the ticket, in addition to an air ticket refund.

SUMMARY

With the maturing of the airline industry, governments are developing policies to protect consumers' rights, and two major policy makers are the European Union and the US Department of Transport. Airline associations have also developed a set of rules for its members. The consumer protection law is written to protect the consumers' right concerning ticket purchase, transparency of information disseminated and the regulation of airline procedures and compensations during instances of flight disruption, such as denied boarding, delay and cancellation. There is also a set of rules protecting customers' baggage and personal belongings.

APPLYING THE KNOWLEDGE

1. Why do governments pass consumer protection laws governing the airline industry? Write your answers in complete sentences. Are passengers protected by the consumer protection law in these scenarios? Read the statements below and put a tick in the correct box.

Statement	Yes	No
1. I am concerned that the airline is not transparent in releasing information about air fares and travel dates.		
2. Will the airline penalize me for changing my reservation?		
3. Are there hidden charges in my ticket?		
4. I need to use a wheelchair on board the aircraft.		
5. The airline staff told me that I do not have a seat on the flight even though my reservation is confirmed.		
6. Will I have to pay extra for checked bags and an assigned seat of my choice?		
7. What will I be compensated if my flight is cancelled?		
8. There are multiple fares available for me to choose from on the website.		
9. The airline has lost my baggage.		
10. I would like to file a complaint for the bad service I received from the cabin crew.		
11. My flight is delayed and the airline offered me food and drinks on board the aircraft.		
12. The airline has sent me a text message informing that my flight time has been changed from 0600 to 0925.		
13. The reservation staff informed me that I will be taking a flight with their code-share partner.		
14. The airline I purchase my air ticket from went bankrupt.		
15. During a delay, the cabin crew made an announcement informing us that we can choose to deplane and return to the airport terminal.		

ENDNOTES

1. International Air Transportation Association. (2013). Passenger rights. International Air transportation Association: https://www.iata.org/policy/Documents/passenger-rights.pdf
2. Department of Transportation, United States. (2016). Airline customer service plan. Department of Transportation, United States: http://airconsumer.ost.dot.gov/customerservice.htm

3. Department of Transportation, United States. (2009, DEC 21). New DOT Consumer Rule Limits Airline Tarmac Delays, Provides Other Passenger Protections. Department of Transportation, United States: http://www.transportation.gov/briefing-room/new-dot-consumer-rule-limits-airline-tarmac-delays-provides-other-passenger#sthash.SuBRD3A8.dpuf

4. European Union Law. (2004, FEB 11). Regulation (EC) No 261/2004 of the European Parliament and of the Council of 11 February 2004 establishing common rules on compensation and assistance to passengers in the event of denied boarding and of cancellation or long delay of flights, and repealing Regulation (EEC) No 295/91 (Text with EEA relevance)—Commission Statement. European Union Law.: http://eur-lex.europa.eu/legal-content/EN/TXT/?uri=CELEX:32004R0261

5. International Air Transportation Association. (2016). Resolution on IATA core principles on consumer protection. International Air Transportation Association: http://www.iata.org/pressroom/pr/Documents/agm69-resolution-passenger-rights.pdf

6. Department of Transportation, United States of America (2006) Follow up review: performance of U.S airlines in implementing selected provision of the airline customer service commitment.

7. European Union. (2016, JUN 13). Air passenger rights. European Union: http://europa.eu/youreurope/citizens/travel/passenger-rights/air/index_en.htm

8. U.S. Government Publishing Office. (2016, Sep 7). §250.8 Denied boarding compensation. U.S. Government Publishing Office: http://www.ecfr.gov/cgi-bin/retrieveECFR?gp=&r=PART&n=14y4.0.1.1.30

9. Airport of Thailand. (2010). Announcement of the Ministry of Transport on Protection of Passenger Rights Using Thai Carriers' Services for Domestic Scheduled Routes. Ministry of Transport: https://airportthai.co.th/uploads/profiles/0000000002/filemanager/files/articleen_20121219103505(1).pdf

10. Li, M. (2010, Nov 2). New rules of China airlines to pay passengers in cash for delay. People Daily Online: http://en.people.cn/90001/90776/90882/7185323.html

11. Directorate General of Civil Aviation, India. (2014, Apr 1), 3.5 Compensation, Directorate General of Civil Aviation, India: http://www.dgca.nic.in/

CHAPTER SIX

Understanding Customer Behavior

Chapter Outline

Learning Objectives

After reading this chapter, the reader should be able to:
- Understand various customers' characteristics
- Recognize the impact of culture on customer behavior
- Identify different customers based on their religious behavior

INTERPRETING CUSTOMER BEHAVIOR

Today's airline service agents interact with customers from different countries and of different nationalities and culture. One of the biggest challenges for service agents is to attend to customers of different backgrounds and personalities. Every customer is different in how they interact with service agents, and this translates to how they gather information, evaluate problems and make decisions. As such, service agents must be able to identify customers' personality during the interaction so that they can offer the appropriate personalized services.

Customers' characteristics

Airline customers can be divided into four different categories of which, each has its unique set of characteristics. It is important for airline frontline service agent to be able to distinguish these customer categories so as to best attend to these customers' needs or requests.

- **Leisure travelers** travel for pleasure and are generally excited about their trips. More often than not, these customers travel in groups or with family members, including elderly and small kids. Frontline service agents need to show interest in their travel plans and offer assistance to the elderly and young travelers when necessary. A casual tone of voice can sometimes be used to create relax and fun conversations.
- **Business travelers** travel very often, and they are usually familiar with the job duties and responsibilities of airline frontline service agents. They expect service agents to be efficient and knowledgeable and to be able to resolve their problems promptly. Their main concerns are

on-time departure and arrival. In addition, a formal tone of voice is usually preferred to demonstrate respect for these customers.

○ **Customers who travel due to emergencies** are usually in a hurry to fly to a destination for specific purposes, and will appreciate that frontline service agents show some form of care. A caring tone of voice is used to demonstrate concern and empathy.

○ **Frequent flyers** are customers who fly frequently. They expect airline frontline service agents to be knowledgeable and to be able to give sound advice when problems occur. In addition, these travelers are fully aware of the benefits that they are entitled to, what service agents can offer and their bottom line. As such, service agents need to be able to sense these customers' attitude during interactions and can use either a causal or formal tone of voice, depending on the situation.

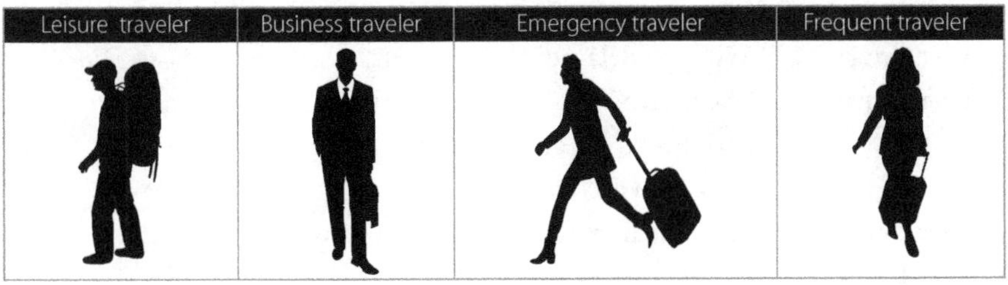

| Leisure traveler | Business traveler | Emergency traveler | Frequent traveler |

Figure 6-1: Types of customers.

Personality types

In 1928, Swiss psychiatrist, Carl Jung identified four groups of people based on how they process information: thinkers, sensors, feelers, and intuitors.[1] In 1985, Rebecca Morgan renamed them as follows: detail seeker, results seeker, excitement seekers, and harmony seekers.[2]

Detail seekers

These customers think logically, are detail oriented, and usually expect a thorough explanation of any process. Detail seekers are usually willing to wait patiently for airline service agents to seek others' advice for clarification to their questions. However, they have zero tolerance for mistakes and expect honest, direct answers. After receiving all the necessary details, these customers will then take time to compare alternatives and make a decision based on the most favorable option available.

Below are some useful tips and techniques when interacting with detail seekers:

- Show care and concern
- Provide accurate facts and data
- Include as much details as possible
- Speak slowly and allow time for customers to analyze the information
- Possible to engage in logical arguments when the need arises

Check-in agent:	I am sorry, Mr. Smith. The flight has been delayed for two hours.
Customer:	Why is it delayed?
Check-in agent:	The delay is caused by bad weather conditions in Tokyo, and this flight is operated by an aircraft that is usually docked in Tokyo.
Customer:	Has that aircraft departed from Tokyo?
Check-in agent:	Yes, it is on the way.
Customer:	What time will it arrive?
Check-in agent:	The flight is scheduled to arrive at 1:30 pm, and will depart at 3 pm.
Customer:	Are there any other options?
Check-in agent:	Yes, Mr. Smith. XX Airline has another flight that will depart for Tokyo at 1455hr, i.e. 5 minutes earlier than your updated flight schedule. However, it will arrive at Narita International Airport slightly later.
Customer:	How can that possible?
Check-in agent:	They are flying a smaller aircraft, Mr. Smith.
Customer:	I see. Thanks for the information. I prefer to stick to the original flight then. Thank you.

Results seekers

Similar to detail seekers, result seekers have zero tolerance for mistakes. These customers are concerned about time and they expect the entire check-in process to be completed quickly. In addition, they usually do not take well to being given advice as they are sure about what they are doing, and will even give out instructions to others. Result seekers are fast decision-makers and they expect service agents to provide accurate information without any delay. At times, these customers can be forceful and demanding. These customers also tend to show off their authority in front of others.

Below are some useful tips and techniques when interacting with result seekers:

- Do due diligence before replying to queries
- Offering a straightforward response
- Reply straight to the point and keep the information short and concise
- Show confidence when stating point of view, and without challenging customers' authority
- Explain the result benefits
- Provide two or more options to allow customers to make their own decisions

Check-in agent:	I am sorry, Mr. Smith. The flight has been delayed for two hours.
Customer:	Why is it delayed?
Check-in agent:	The delay is caused by bad weather conditions in Tokyo, and this flight is operated by an aircraft that is usually docked in Tokyo.
Customer:	Put me on another flight.
Check-in agent:	Yes, Mr. Smith. XX Airline has another flight that will depart for Tokyo at 1455hr, i.e. 5 minutes earlier than your updated flight schedule. However, it will arrive at Narita International Airport slightly later. Which do you prefer?
Customer:	I see. Please put me on XX Airline's flight.
Check-in agent:	Certainly, Mr. Smith.

Excitement seekers

These customers are usually creative, fun-loving, enthusiastic, and idealistic, and are great conversationalists. More often than not, they are disorganized and tend to jump from one activity to another, and get bored easily. Excitement seekers like to be involved and detest being alone. They also seek social approval and like to exaggerate as so to get attention and approval from others. These customers generally raise their voices when they talk in order to get another attention.

Below are some useful tips and techniques for interacting with result seekers:

- Allow them to talk
- Show respect so as to build trust
- Show personalized care
- Treat them as a friend
- Use jokes when appropriate to diffuse tense situations

Check-in agent:	I am sorry, Mr. Smith. The flight has been delayed for two hours.
Customer:	What? It is delayed again? I've taken this flight many times and it is delayed 80% of the time. So, what's the cause of delay this time?
Check-in agent:	The delay is caused by bad weather conditions in Tokyo, and this flight is operated by an aircraft that is usually docked in Tokyo.
Customer:	Geez! You know what, I think your company should simply reschedule this flight as it is always delayed!
Check-in agent:	Yes, I agree. I wish I own this company. In fact, I'll fly you to Tokyo by myself if I were the pilot!
Customer:	I really appreciated that, but I don't trust your flying skills. Hahaha.
Check-in agent:	Haha. I know! Well … Mr. Smith, here is your boarding pass.

Harmony seekers

Harmony seekers like to interact with others and care about how they feel. However, these customers are slow decision-makers as they do not like to take the initiative in a situation. They usually wait for others to provide them suggestions and will often seek alternative recommendations. They also tend to avoid conflicts with others.

Below are some useful tips and techniques for interacting with harmony seekers:

- Be friendly
- Offer multiple options and help these customers to make the best decision whenever possible
- Do not take advantage of their easy-going personality
- Show empathy and understanding

Check-in agent: I am sorry, Mr. Smith. The flight has been delayed for two hours.

Customer: Oh, why is it delayed?

Check-in agent: The delay is caused by bad weather conditions in Tokyo, and this flight is operated by an aircraft that is usually docked in Tokyo.

Customer: Oh dear! Are there any other alternatives?

Check-in agent: Yes, Mr. Smith. XX Airline has another flight that will depart for Tokyo at 1455 hr, i.e. 5 minutes earlier than your updated flight schedule. However, it will arrive at Narita International Airport slightly later.

Customer: Hmm … I'm not sure if I should opt for the other flight. What do you think?

Check-in agent: Mr. Smith, I am sure you will find that our service and in-flight entertainment are much better than the other airlines. You will arrive at Narita International Airport slightly earlier too.

Customer: You're right. I'll take your word for it. Can you please help me to check in?

CULTURE INFLUENCES ON CUSTOMER BEHAVIOR

Customers of different nationalities differ in their behavior and may have peculiar expectations. Due to cultural differences, these customers may react to the same problem differently. Below are some observations of different ethnic groups.

Africans

Africans refer to individuals who are either natives or inhabitants of Africa. This also extends to a person and especially a black person of African ancestry. While there are many different tribes in the African continent and each has its own unique set of behavior, many Africans are influenced by mainstream Western European culture. African customers have a tendency to exercise self-control; they are always careful not to upset or embarrass anyone in public and also expect the same in return. These customers usually prefer harmonious interactions and make an effort to avoid any sort of confrontation. In addition, the idea of one's personal space is less important for Africans—they often don't mind being physically close when engaging in conversations.[3]

On the other hand, a large number of Africans have migrated to the United States in the 17th century. They tend to behave differently as compared to native Africans due to the influence of Western culture and these groups of people are known as African Americans.[4] It is not easy to distinguish these two groups solely based on their appearance.

Ethnicity	General characteristics
Native Africans	• Punctually is not deemed important • Important to maintain good eye contact when greeting or speaking with others • Never stare at others • Avoid getting overly upset or frustrated with others
African Americans/ Africans in European	• Shake hands when meeting (both men and women) • Direct eye contact is necessary • Punctually is critical • Prefer direct communication
South Africans	• Maintain eye contact and smile while shaking hands • Avoid confrontations • Do not interrupt them when they are speaking • Punctuality is important to English-speaking South Africans, while others tend to be more flexible with the concept of time

Westerners

Western culture, sometimes equated with Western civilization, Western lifestyle or European civilization, is a term used very broadly to refer to a heritage of social norms, ethical values, traditional customs, belief systems, political systems, and specific artifacts and technologies that have some origin or association with Europe. This term is applicable to countries whose history are strongly marked by European immigration, such as the countries of the Americas and Australasia, and is not restricted to the continent of Europe. This includes countries in Europe as well as the United States where Europeans settled during the 16th century,[5] and Australia in the 18th century.[6]

Today, Western cultures have influences in many countries around the world. In spite of this, there are still some obvious differences among the different nationalities. The following are some general characteristics of Westerners. These customers value individualism and expect to be treated equally while given special attention by the service agents at same time. Timeliness is of concern to those customers and they assume that everything is taking place according to schedule. Customers who are brought up in a Western culture also place emphasis on logic and expect service agents to speak clearly and to go straight to the point. These customers are not afraid of confrontation; they will voice out their opinion when something is amiss. They also expect others to behave in the same way as they do.

Nationality	General characteristics
American[7]	• Passionate about freedom of choice and speech • Need personal space • Punctual • Follow rules and law • Maintain eye contact and smile during conversation
Australian	• Casual and informal • Communicate using direct language • Show respect by others in the eye • Need personal space • Good sense of humor • Acceptable to show anger and emotions in public

(Continued)

Nationality	General characteristics
British	• Polite • Need personal space • Punctual • Follow rules and regulations • Sarcastic and self-depreciating sense of humor
German	• Hardworking, efficient and disciplined • Love planning schedules • Punctual • Problem solvers • Do not give up without a solution
Russian	• Restrained in public • Time is not important • Patient • Reserved and toned-down • Subscribe to high-context cultures
South American	• Attitude toward time is less rigid • Usually stand closer to others during conversation • Enjoy social conversations

Arabs

Arab cultures refer to the culture of the Arabs and generally extend to countries where Arabic is the dominant language. The Arab world stretches from Morocco across Northern Africa to the Persian Gulf, and is also commonly known as the Middle East and North Africa (MENA).

Arabs usually do not like open criticism and will often go around the bush just to get a message across. As such, service agents must read between the lines in order to get the actual meaning and gist of a message. These customers do not like to be hurried, and mistrust can be developed when agents do not give these customers enough time to make decisions. Arabs are very relaxed about the concept of time and do not place much importance on timeliness. They also enjoy lengthy conversations and have a tendency to speak in a louder voice as a loud volume, increased pitch and tone are indications of honesty. In addition, maintaining eye contact during interactions demonstrates sincerity and honor—Arabs judge one's ability by his or her ability to maintain strong eye contact.[8] Arabs of the same gender also generally stand very close to one another when they have a conversation. On the other hand, leaning against the wall or keeping one's hands in pocket during a conversation is a sign of disrespect.

Nationality	General characteristics
Algerian	• Avoid any forms of physical contact • Important to maintain eye contact when speaking • Frequent use of hand gestures when speaking • Avoid contradicting others in public • Punctuality is not very important
Egyptian	• People of same gender keep a close distance, people of opposite gender maintain a distance from each other • Speak loudly during argument • Shake hands very often • Public display of anger is discouraged
Emirati	• Prefer indirect communication • Place emphasis on face-saving behavior • People of same gender keep a close distance, people of opposite gender maintain a distance from each other • Do not like conflicts
Saudi Arabian	• Friendly and sociable • Maintain eye contact during conversation • Physical contact with the opposite gender is prohibited • Reserved emotions in public • Usually increase voice volume during conversation
Somalian	• People of opposite gender maintain a distance from each other • Do not establish direct eye contact • Speak loudly • Like to join in other people's conversations • Not obsessed about time

Asians

Asian culture is diverse and rich in cultural heritage, and comprises many nationalities, societies, and ethnic groups in the Asia continent. The continent is divided into natural geographic and cultural sub-regions, including Central Asia, East Asia, North Asia, South Asia, Southeast Asia and West Asia. Many of these Asian cultures are influenced by Western culture as a result of colonization. For example, British influence in Myanmar, Malaysia, Singapore and Hong Kong; French influence in Cambodia, Laos and Vietnam; and US influence in the Philippines.

In some Asian cultures, eye contact is considered inappropriate as it can be interpreted as a sign of disrespect. Most Asians are indirect communicators, i.e. a verbal message may have a different intended meaning. When communicating with Asian customers, service agents must speak carefully to avoid making customers lose face. The concept of face or *mianzi* idiomatically refers to one's own sense of dignity, reputation and prestige. In addition, silence is generally prefer as a means of avoiding confrontation as it is considered rude to speak up in public, especially in face of higher authorities. However, there are some exceptions to the norm; Chinese and India customers are generally more opinionated and tend to speak more loudly due to the respective countries' competitive cultures.

In this new era of globalization, many Asians have moved and settled down in various Western countries. As such, they may have adopted and internalized Western cultural norms over time. For example, US Chinese citizens may react to a certain situation very differently from a Chinese national based in Shanghai.

Nationality	General characteristics
Cambodian	• Avoid maintaining eye contact during conversations • Use soft tone of voice • Minimum gestures when speaking • Laughing or making jokes are acceptable
Chinese	• Comfortable with personal zone distance • Maintain eye contact during conversation • Speak loudly • Rely on implicit communication and non-verbal cues • May be aggressive • Places importance on face/*mianzi*
Filipino	• Warm and hospitable • Use a lot of non-verbal communication during conversations, e.g. raising eyebrows or lifting the head upwards slightly to indicate "yes" or to greet friends • Avoid confrontation • Avoid expressing anger in public
Indonesian	• Direct eye contact should be avoided • Rely on implicit communication and non-verbal cues • Places importance on face/*mianzi* • Avoid touching the other people when talking • Never use left hand to give or receive things
Japanese	• Acceptable distance depends on the space between individuals • Any form of physical contact is unwelcomed • Occasionally maintain eye contact • Tendency to use indirect forms of communication • Rare public displays of emotion

(Continued)

Nationality	General characteristics
Lao people	• Keep a distance when talking • Not important to maintain eye contact during conversation • Minimal gestures while speaking • Public displays of anger are considered shameful and embarrassing • Generally flexible about timeliness and punctuality; varies according to individuals
Malaysian	• Keep an appropriate distance during conversation • Friendly but reserved • Not important to maintain eye contact during conversation • Volume and tone of voice may increase or change when excited
Singaporean	• Very informal • Reserved • Moderate tone of voice; speaking loudly in public is considered rude • Rare public displays of emotion and anger • Most arguments are expected to be resolved in private
South Korean	• Eye contact is avoided during conversations • Do not use gestures when speaking • Tone of voice is generally soft, gentle and polite • Public displays of anger are not generally accepted • Pay attention to timeliness and punctuality
Taiwanese	• Very understanding and inquisitive • Maintain eye contact during conversation • Limited facial expressions • Openly show dissatisfaction with product or service of poor quality and demand improvement or explanation for said product or service • Speaking loudly in public is considered rude
Thai	• Maintain eye contact during conversation • Rarely express anger • Public displays of emotions are only displayed to close friends and family • Not particular about timeliness and punctuality • Do not plan ahead of time
Vietnamese	• Maintain a distance from others when speaking • Do not necessarily maintain constant eye contact during conversation • Express feelings of anger or happiness in public • Loud tone of voice demonstrates anger • Not particular about timeliness and punctuality

Eastern vs. Western passengers

A service agent at the boarding gate had just made an announcement to inform that a flight has been delayed. As soon as the announcement has been made, all the Asian customers rushed to the boarding gate's podium and formed a crowd around the podium, which was mended by one service agent. The service agent was flooded with questions.

On another flight comprising of only Western passengers, the customers formed an orderly line at the podium and waited for their turn to ask the service agent questions.

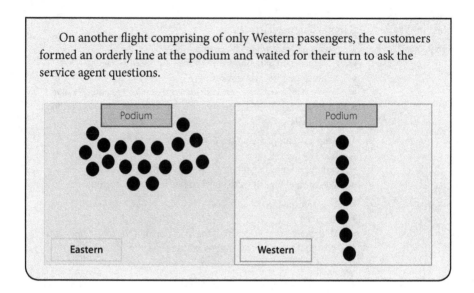

RELIGIOUS BEHAVIOR

Behavior is very much influenced by religious beliefs. Religion is a collection of belief and cultural system that affects a person's action, and some customers' dietary practices are a result of their religious beliefs. As such, service agents need to be pay attention to customers' religions so as to avoid any misunderstanding.

Christianity

Christianity is the major region in many Western countries and it is the most popular religion in the world with over two billion followers. Christianity originates in the Middle East and is then spread to Europe and other parts of the world. Christians are free to consume any food and beverages. Christian priests and nuns can be identified by their clerical collar-coif (a woman's close-fitting cap, worn under a veil by nuns) and guimpe (a high-necked blouse or undergarment worn showing beneath a low-necked dress).

Christians are not subjected to any dietary restrictions. However, some Christians have adopted a policy of Christian vegetarianism.

Buddhism

Buddhism is a major religion in the Eastern hemisphere. Buddhism started in northern India and later spread eastward to other Asian countries.[9] Buddhist monks and nuns are subjected to strict codes of conduct-they must not have any physical contact with someone of the opposite gender and they are not allowed to consume any alcohol. Some pious Buddhist believers also keep to these codes of conduct.

Buddhist monks and nuns adopt specific dietary practices in different Asian countries. Monks and nuns who practice Theravada Buddhism only eat in the mornings and before noontime. They are allowed to eat anything offered by others but are prohibited from consuming alcohol. Theravada Buddhism monks and nuns are commonly found in Sri Lanka, Thailand, Cambodia, Laos and Myanmar. Theravada monks are identified by their red or yellow robes.

On the other hand, monks in China, Vietnam, Korea and Japan are strictly vegetarian and do not consume dairy products. All vegetarian dishes prepared must exclude alliums vegetables such as onions, leeks, garlic, scallions and ginger. Monk and nuns from these areas usually wear yellow, grey or black robes.[10]

Airline service agents must be made aware of these special customers and the code of conduct that they are subjected to. Service agents must ensure monks or nuns are not seated next to another customer of the opposite gender. A cabin crew of the same gender should also offer beverage or meals to these customers. If a cabin crew of the same gender is not available on a particular flight, the cabin crew must pay attention not to have direct contact with the monk or nun while offering in-flight service.

Islam

Islam is the world's second-largest religion and the fastest-growing major religion in the world, with over 1.8 billion followers to date. It originates in Mecca and spread to other parts of the world. Muslims are people who have professed belief in Islam. According to the Quran, Muslims are forbidden from consuming any pork, blood and alcoholic beverages.[11]

Muslim women are also not allowed to socialize with anyone of the opposite gender unless he is a close relative. As such, when making travel arrangements for a Muslim woman who is traveling alone, service agents should always try and allocate appropriate seats for the customer.[12] When offering in-flight services to such customers, service staff should take care not to offend Muslim customers or make them feel uncomfortable in any way.

Hinduism

Hinduism, also known as the oldest religion in the world, is practiced mostly in India, Mauritius and Nepal. Due to the British colonization, Hinduism has also spread to other countries such as Singapore and Malaysia.[13]

Hinduism believers are forbidden to eat meat, poultry, fish or eggs. In addition, consumption of beef strictly forbidden is not allowed as cows are thought to be sacred animals and are deeply respected.

Judaism

Orthodox Jewish customers with religious belief in Judaism are subjected to very strict dietary restrictions and are only allowed to consume food that are kosher and conform to the regulations of kashrut (Jewish dietary law).

Kosher in-flight meals need to be ordered in advance and are specially prepared under certain rules. For example, meat and dairy must be completely separated during food preparation and kosher kitchens must contain separate sets of utensils and preparation areas to ensure that dairy products and meat are not served on the same table.[14]

CLOTHING AND EMOTIONAL COLORS

Service agents may sometimes be able to identify customers' religious beliefs based on their outfit. The standard Muslim male clothing attire covers the shoulders and torso and legs, and extends from the navel to the knees while standard Muslim female clothing covers the entire body, with the exception of one's face and hands.[15]

Male Judaism customers can be easily recognized by their kippah, a small brimless cap, usually made of cloth and worn by Jewish males.

Customers' choice of clothing color can also sometimes give hints to their behavior as colors can help to reveal a person's mood and behavior.[16]

Color	Behavioral cues
Black	protective, formal, completeness, independent
Blue	trusting, orderly, caring, shows concern
Brown	practical, approachable, friendly, stable
Green	self-reliant, calm, practical, caring
Greenish-Blue	creative, harmonious, idealistic, calm
Grey	reliable, professional, intelligent, calm
Indigo	organized, responsible, honest, practical
Orange	sociable, optimistic, self-confident, independent
Pink	understanding, warm, calm, feminine
Purple	creative, daydreams, original, kind
Purplish-red	harmonious, emotionally balanced, logical, supportive, kind
Red	excited, power hungry, energetic, fast
White	fair, impartial, neat, simple, open-minded
Yellow	warm, cheerful, enthusiastic, fun-loving

OTHER BEHAVIOR

Baby boomers

Baby boomers are older customers and usually refer to those who are between 50 and 60 years old. Due to the surging birth rate in the post World War II period between 1946 and 1964, there are approximately 1.4 billion baby boomers worldwide as of in 2015.[17] These customers have high purchasing power and the money and time for travel. They are usually slow in making decisions and some might be suffering from presbyopia-long-sightedness caused by loss of elasticity of the lens

Figure 6-2: Religious costumes help service agents to identify customers' religious beliefs.

of the eye, occurring typically in middle and old age. As such, they may have difficulty reading words in fine print or have problems hearing. These customers expect service agents to show them respect and give them extra attention. Service agents can ensure a smooth interaction with these customers by being more patient and spending additional time to satisfy their needs and demands.

Millennials/generation Y

This refers to the generation of people born during the 1980s and early 1990s, i.e. customers who are between the ages of 20 and 35. This group of customers relies heavily on technology and prefers to communicate via technology as opposed to face-to-face communication. When serving millennials, service agents should endeavor to keep the message short and brief whilst providing concise and accurate details as these customers usually have already done their research online before seeking assistance from service agents.

Customer with special needs

Service agents must be very careful when interacting with these customers so as to avoid any potential conflicts or misunderstanding. Service agents should not assume that all special needs customers need help. It is best to ask these customers if they require any assistance first before offering a helping hand. If these customers travel with a companion, it is disrespectful to only talk to the passenger's companion and assume he or she will help to pass on the message. When communicating with passengers on wheelchairs, service agents should speak to them at eye level. Service agents should always bend down to the customer's level whenever possible. It is also not appropriate to play with these passengers' guide dogs.

LGBTQ customers

LGBTQ is an initialism that stands for lesbian, gay, bisexual, transgender and queer. These customers are more often than not, sensitive about being treated equally and expect service agents to respect their lifestyles. Service agents must not discriminate these customers in any way and should offer the same quality and standard of service as they would to the other customers.

SUMMARY

Customer behavior is influenced by a variety of factors. This includes race, culture, religion and purpose of travel. Business travelers are concerned about timeliness while leisure travels pay more attention to the cost of air tickets. Rebecca Morgan identified the following four common personality types: detail seekers, results seekers, excitement seekers and harmony seekers. It is important for airline frontline staff to be able to identify passengers of different cultures and religions so as to offer appropriate services to these customers.

APPLYING THE KNOWLEDGE

True or false?
Are the following statements true or false? Put a tick in the right column.

Statement	True	False
1. Detail seekers do not think logically and do not pay attention to small details.		
2. Result seeks are patient and tolerant of others' mistakes.		
3. Excitement seekers are creative and enthusiastic.		
4. Harmony seekers are individuals that prefer to stay away from groups of people.		
5. Many Africans are fluent in English and French.		
6. Western culture refers to countries that are closely related to Europe.		
7. In some Asian cultures, it is disrespectful to maintain eye contact during conversations.		
8. A Muslim customer is forbidden to consume pork or alcohol.		
9. Kosher food is a special cuisine that is prepared for Hindu customers.		
10. All Vietnamese monks are vegetarians.		

Short-answer questions

1. You are a service agent helping a Chinese passenger to check in for his flight from Shanghai to Japan. The passenger's name is Zhang Zilian. You notice that the passenger looks annoyed after you addressed him as Mr. Zilian. What went wrong?
2. You are a male service agent. You have just helped a female Malaysian customer to rebook her flight. After the customer thanked you, you shook her hand as a gesture of friendliness. You then noticed that the customer looked uncomfortable and tried to pull her hand away. What went wrong?
3. You are a female service agent stationed at the boarding gate. You notice that a Buddhist monk has accidentally tripped on a bag left by another customer. What should you do?
4. You are a male check-in agent for a flight to Saudi Arabia. A female Saudi Arabian passenger dressed in a black abaya and head scarf approaches you to check in for her flight. As part of the check-in procedure, you are required to match the photo on her passport with her face. What should you do?

ENDNOTES

1. Field, G. (1998). Human behavior in organizations: a Canadian perspective Prentice Hall Canada.
2. Morgan, R. (2012). Professional Selling. rebeccamorgan.com: www.rebeccamorgan.com/articles/selling/selling1.html
3. Wien, M. (2011, Mar 28). 17 African Cultural Values (To Know Before You Travel to Africa). Migrationology.com http://migrationology.com/2011/03/african-cultural-values-travel-africa-17/
4. History. (2015). SLAVERY IN AMERICA. History.com: http://www.history.com/topics/black-history/slavery
5. Florida Departmet of State. (2015). 16th Century Settlements. Florida department of state: http://dos.myflorida.com/florida-facts/florida-history/16th-century-settlements/

6. Davison, G., Hirst, J. and MacIntyre, S. (2011). Convicts and the British colonies in Australia, Australian government: http://www.australia.gov.au/about-australia/australian-story/convicts-and-the-british-colonies

7. University of Michigan Press. (2015). 101 Characteristics of Americans/American Culture. University of Michigan Press: https://www.press.umich.edu/pdf/9780472033041-101AmerCult.pdf

8. IOR Global Service. (2015). Cultural Insights: United Arab Emirates (UAE). IOR Global Service: http://www.iorworld.com/united-arab-emirates-cultural-insights—worldview—cultural-assumptions—communication-style—business-practices-pages-483.php

9. About Buddhism. (2007). History of Buddhism. About Buddhism: http://www.aboutbuddhism.org/history-of-buddhism.htm/

10. Wei, C. (2013, Feb 13). ACTOID #2: WHY CHINESE BUDDHIST VEGETARIANS DON'T EAT GARLIC. Clasrissa: http://clarissawei.com/2013/02/13/factoid-2-why-chinese-buddhist-vegetarians-dont-eat-garlic/

11. Ismail, M. (2012). Islamic Dress for Men. Muslim Network of Podcasts and Blogs: http://islamiclearningmaterials.com/islamic-dress-for-men/

12. Hammond, P. (2012, Jun 23). Religious dietary guidelines and restrictions, Chewfo: http://www.chewfo.com/philosophical-reasons-for-food-choices/religious-dietary-restrictions/

13. Lai, A. E. (2008). Religious Diversity in Singapore. Institute of Southeast Asian Studies. pp491.

14. Culzac, N. (2014, Aug 18). What is Kosher food? A brief explanation... independent: http://www.independent.co.uk/life-style/food-and-drink/news/what-is-kosher-food-a-brief-explanation-9676266.html

15. Inquisitr. (2015, Jan 2). Saudi Arabia Airline Segregation: New Islamic Law Takes Flight On Airliner, Seating By Gender Coming Soon. Inquisitr: http://www.inquisitr.com/1721945/saudi-arabia-airline-segregation-new-islamic-law-takes-flight-on-airliner-seating-by-gender-coming-soon/#t2DowijfXTlDxIqz.99

16. Cao, J. (2015, Apr 7). Web design color theory: how to create the right emotions with color in web design. TNW.: https://thenextweb.com/dd/2015/04/07/how-to-create-the-right-emotions-with-color-in-web-design/

17. United Nations, Department of Economic and Social Affairs, Population Division (2015). World Population Ageing 2015 (ST/ESA/SER.A/390).

CHAPTER SEVEN

The Airline Customer Contact Centre

Chapter Outline

Learning Objectives

After reading this chapter, the reader should be able to:

- Understand the role and function of airline customer contact center
- Recognize the process of a standard call flow
- Identify various communication skills required of contact center representatives

AIRLINE CUSTOMER CONTACT CENTER

The airline customer contact center is traditionally known as the reservation department, and it serves as one of the main contact points between an airline and its customers. Customers call the airline contact center for a variety of purposes. These include general inquiries, purchasing of tickets, changing of reservations and air ticket refund. The contact center also serves as an airline's customer relations department for handling customer complaints and dealing with both internal and external customers.

Internal customers
- Airline service agents
  - Liaise with service agents from other departments, e.g. customer service representatives from the airport enquiring about passenger-related matters on reservations and ticket fares.
  - Make reservation list and check flight loading and availability of flights for fellow employees for staff's travel purposes.
- Other airline staff
  - Make reservations for passengers of another airline due to irregular operations.
  - Check booking status and ticket status for other airlines.
- Travel agents
  - Attend to enquiries related to passengers' booking issues such as change of names, change of booking details and ticket deadline extensions
  - Handle requests for specific seat assignments
  - Reconfirm booking of flight and special service request status

External passengers
- Airline passengers
  - Attend to general enquiries such as baggage allowance and meals offered, amongst others
  - Handle all matters related to booking and pricing of air tickets, enquiries about space availability on a flight and fare, and make flight reservations.

- ○ Handle queries related to frequent flier programs, and earning and redeeming of air miles
- ○ Make changes to existing reservations
- ○ Handle all complaints

The airline contact center usually has hundreds of workstations that are mended by reservation service agents and each workstation is equipped with a computer and a telephone. Customers can reach the contact center via telephone, website and through social media.

MEANS OF CONTACT

In the past, customers contact airline contact centers solely via phone calls. These days, customers can easily reach reservation service agents via a number of other ways.

Telephone

The traditional contact method is through telecommunication networks, i.e. both internal and external customers contact the airline contact center via the phone. Many airlines today have centralized their contact center, whereby calls are connected to a main call center in the airline's respective county or directed to an office in another country. After a call is connected, it will be directed to a telephone system, known as the Automatic Call Distributor (ACD). This is a system that helps airline call centers to respond to the high volume of incoming calls. The pre-recorded voice in the system will then ask some basic questions and customers need to select their desired services by punching in the corresponding numbers on the telephone number pad. The system then directs these customers to the correct department, and these calls are placed in a queue until they are handled by service agents.

Some airlines also use this telephone system to segregate customer types to ensure the lines will be directed to the right agents so as to improve the waiting time. A number of airlines also dedicate specific telephone numbers based on travel class, while others use the ACD to differentiate various customer types. For example, frequent travelers are required to insert their frequent flyer membership numbers for verification. Once verification has been made, their information will be transferred to service agents who are specially assigned to take care of these loyal customers. This is effective in minimizing the waiting time of these high-yield passengers and to ensure their calls are promptly attended to.

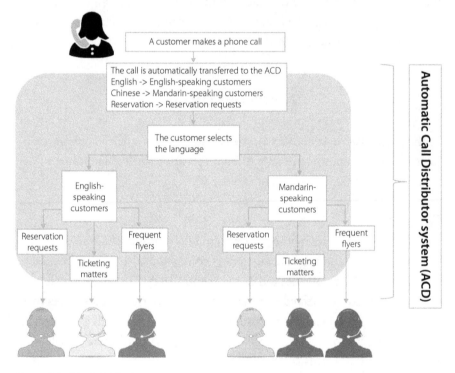

Figure 7-1: A typical airline' system.

To deal with the high volume of phone calls, some airlines have configured their ACD system to allow customers to leave voice messages if they prefer not to remain on hold. The customer contact center's representatives will then respond to these customers' calls within a stipulated period of time.

Website/live chat

Customers may also choose to contact service agents via an airline's website. Most airlines today allow passengers to leave messages on the website and the airline service agent can reply these messages either via email or phone calls. With the advancement in technology, many airlines have also added a real-time chat function, which is also mended by the reservation service agents at the contact center. Passengers can now access an airline's website and select the real-time chat function to request to chat with the airline service agent. Similar to phone calls, these requests will be placed in a queue and they will be served by the next available service agent.

Social media

Social media refers to computer-mediated technologies that facilitate the creation and sharing of information, ideas, career interests and other forms of expression via virtual communities and networks. Many airlines today are catching on the social media trend and are using external communication channels such as Facebook and Twitter to communicate with customers. Customers can easily access an airline's official page on the social media and send a message via the "comment" section. Service agents can either reply directly to any of these comments via social media or contact the passengers by phone in instances where contact numbers are provided or when a particular feedback requires detailed follow-up actions.

Electronic mail (email)

There are many customers who prefer to contact airline contact centers through the use of electronic mail system. As such, most airlines list the email address of the various departments on their official webpage. This helps customers to contact the respective departments based on their requests.

Replying to customers' requests

Customers who leave a message through any of the above-mentioned four channels usually expect service agents to get back to them in a timely manner. According to a survey conducted by Software Advice—a company that provides research and user reviews on software applications—in 2014, majority of customers expect their calls to be returned within 30 minutes.[1] Failure to reply in a timely manner can lead to customer dissatisfaction and airlines losing businesses.

Voice mail responses

There may be occasions when service agents are unable to get through to customers during a follow-up call and are diverted to the customers' voice mailboxes instead. It is important for service agents to leave a clear message in order to avoid any confusion and misinterpretation. Below are some pointers as to how service agents can ensure the intended message is conveyed across effectively.

- Speak slowly and clearly
- Always begin with a greeting, followed by an introduction. The introduction should include the agent's name, airline's name and the purpose of the call
- Proceed to deliver the main message
- Remember to leave the contact number and/or other necessary contact details
- Thank the customer and include a polite sign-off message before ending the call

INCOMING CALL FLOW

Below is a contact center's standard call flow that shows the procedure for all incoming calls.

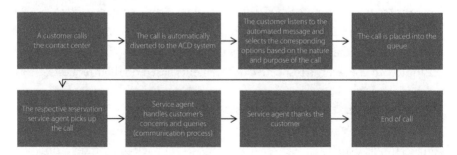

Figure 7-2: Standard call flow.

The following flow applies to customers who contact the airline via other communication channels.

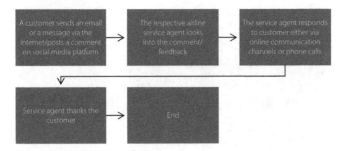

Figure 7-3: Customer contact flow via other communication channels.

ESSENTIAL CUSTOMER SERVICE SKILLS

Both verbal communication and non-verbal communication skills are important when handling customers' queries and concerns. Reservation service agents are sometimes the first point of contact between an airline and its passengers. As such, a memorable and pleasant experience with reservation service agents will often translate to a positive image of the airline. As representatives of the airline customer contact center interact with customers solely via telephone calls and online, these service agents must be superb in both verbal and written communication skills.

Telephone communication

As with all other job functions within an airline, airline reservation service agents must be knowledgeable about the company's products and policies as these forms the bulk of the queries and concerns posed by customers.

Airline service agents are unable to see customers' gestures and facial expressions during a phone call, and it can be difficult to gauge their emotions. Hence, airline service agents need to determine customers' mood via their tone of voice through dialogues. In order to provide excellent services over the telephone, it is important for airline reservation service agents to be able to communicate with customers effectively. This requires outstanding listening skills, speaking skills and problem-solving skills. Reservation service agents must also be prepared to answer all sorts of questions within a short timeframe.

Figure 7-4: A service agent answering a call at the airline reservation center.

Effective communication skills

An effective conversation over the telephone begins with a smile and a sincere greeting. Even though customers are unable to see airline service agents' facial expressions, they can draw conclusions about agents' attitude based on their tone of voice. As such, service agents should always smile when they are on the phone. This is because the soft palate in the back of the mouth rises and makes one's tone more fluid, friendly and approachable.[2] This helps in starting a conversation on a positive note.

Multiple language skills

Proficiency in multiple languages is an extremely valuable asset as this enables service agents to communicate with customers of different nationalities. This is especially so for international airlines whereby customers of different nationalities may contact the center on matters related to purchase of tickets or request for assistance.

Greet customers

Reservation service agents must always show professionalism by greeting customers in a proper manner. This includes a basic greeting, introducing oneself and one's department to the customer, and asking customers how they would like to be assisted.

An example conversation starts with a basic greeting such as "Good morning", "Good afternoon" or "Good evening". There are times when a customer may already be waiting in queue for a long time. As such, an acknowledgement such as "Sorry to keep you waiting." can also be included as part of the greeting message.

Service agents should also introduce themselves to customers so as to build confidence and create a sense of rapport. This is followed by the actual conversation in which service agents then ask customers about the purpose of their calls. This is illustrated in the dialogues below:

Service agent:	Good morning. My name is Vivian from the ticketing department. How can I help you today?
	Good morning. Sorry to keep you waiting. My name is Vivian. How can I help you today?

Positive tone of voice

When speaking to customers, service agents need to maintain high professional standards. This is demonstrated through excellent etiquette and using appropriate speech pace rate as these can convey different means, as mentioned in Chapter 2—"Theory of Communication".

Speaking too fast shows that the service agent is rushing through the conversation and customers may not understand the message. On the other hand, speaking too slowly may be an indication to customers that the service agent is bored and disinterested in the conversation. According to the National Center for Voice and Speech, the average speaking rate for English speakers in the United States is about 150 words per minute.[3] However, when dealing with customers who are not English native speakers, service agents should pace themselves according as these customers may need additional time to decode the messages.

Using simple words and a clear accent

As discussed in Chapter 2, service agents should avoid using complicated vocabulary words and keep their sentences as simple as possible. Service agents are also advised against using slangs or jargons as these can often be confusing and misleading for customers who are not familiar with the airline industry. Filler words—meaningless words, phrases, or sounds that marks a pause or hesitation in speech, such as "um", "uh" and "ah" should also be avoided as these affect the overall quality of the conversation as receivers have a tendency to focus on these words and phrases, and they often draw attention away from the original message. The use of such words and may even create a negative impression as this demonstrates a lack of professionalism. Below are some examples of common sentences with filler words.

Filler word/ phrase	Commonly used by …	Example	What this implies
Really	Native English speakers	Really? This is what the travel agent has told you?	Not believing what the customer has said
I guess		I guess the flight is full.	Uncertainty
I mean		I mean the flight only has a few available seats left.	This is usually used to explain or correct a statement. It may imply that the service agent is not entirely sure.
Quite		The ticket will be quite expensive.	The word "quite" does not reflect the actual value of the ticket, but rather the speaker's personal judgement
Anu	Indonesians	Anu …	Equivalent of "Um …" in English
Ano あ の	Japanese	Ano …	Equivalent of "Um …" in English
Lah	Singaporeans	No problem, lah!	Combining dialect with English creates confusion
Na Ka นะค่ะ/ **Na Krub** นะครับ	Thai nationals	Thank you, na ka!	Combining Thai and English creates confusion

Airline service agents should refrain from using local accent when communicating over the phone to avoid any misunderstanding. The only exception is when it is obvious that a customer understands and very much prefers to speak to a service agent who has the same accent. For English speakers, global or accent-neutral English should be used as the standard. In cities such as Bangkok and Phuket, the Thai language is used. However, service agent should avoid speaking in Southern dialogue, different accent or a dialect that deviates from the standard Thai.

Address customers by name

After greeting customers, service agents should introduce their names and find out that they need. When doing so, service agents should allow time for customers to express their thoughts. It is also good practice to ask customers for their names before making a response. This allows service agents to offer personalized services as addressing customers by their name can help to attract their attention and trust.[4]

Apologize

There are times where service agents may need to put customers on hold while they check for relevant information or make a booking. Upon returning to the call, they should apologize for keeping the customers on hold and keep them updated on what has been to resolve their issues.

Service agent: Mr. Jonathan, I'm sorry to have kept you waiting. I am still preparing your reservation. Could you please hold on the line for another moment? Thank you.

In instances whereby customers need to be put on hold for an extended period of time, service agents need to inform them that they are still addressing their concerns and request for them to wait a while longer.

Service agent: Mr. Jonathan, I'm sorry to have kept you waiting. I have already confirmed your flight for CM 889 from Penang to Krabi on 13 July. The flight will depart at 0920 hr, local time in Malaysia, and arrive at 0920 hr, local time in Thailand.

End on a high note

After providing the necessary information and sorting out customers' problems, airline service agents can end the call by asking customers if there are other issues they can help with. This allows customers to raise other enquires or concerns before the end of the phone call. Service agents should also provide the necessary contact details and any other related information if a needs to call back at a later time to follow up on an enquiry. Last but not least, always wait for customers to hang up after the end of the conversation as this demonstrates respect and patience.

A service agent's care and compassion

A customer called the airline contact center as she desperately needed to fly back home to Sydney as her mother has been admitted to the hospital and was in critical condition. As it was during the high travel season, all flights were fully booked. The service agent at the contact center was unable to secure a flight for the next 10 days and advised the customer to go to the airport directly and try her luck in getting a standby ticket. The customer was disappointed but had no choice but to make her way to the airport in person.

Thirty minutes later, the service agent called and informed the customer that he managed to confirm a seat on a flight that will be depart from Hong Kong in 5 hours. The customer was extremely relieved and touched by the service agent's display of care and compassion.

Service agent:	Miss Alice, is there anything else I can help you with?
Customer:	That is all for today. I will call back tomorrow once I have confirmed my travel schedule.
Service agent:	Sure. Please call us during our office hours between 9 am to 5 pm, Monday to Friday.
Customer:	Great! Thank you for the information.
Service agent:	Once again, thank you for calling C&M Airline. It was nice speaking to you and we look forward to serving you again. Have a good day!
Customer:	It was great speaking to you too. Bye! [hangs up the phone]
Service agent:	[hangs up the phone]

Live chat

It is becoming increasingly common for airlines to include a live chat function on their website as this allows customers to contact them much more easily. Live chat is also a convenient means of communication as it allows customers to contact airline service agents at any time and from anywhere using their cell phones.

Jetstar ★

Newsroom

Melbourne, 13 March 2013

Jetstar introduces web chat service for customers

- Jetstar launches live chat service to answer customer queries
- Live chat links service agents with customers via instant messaging
- Introduction follows a successful trial of live chat for Jetstar holiday bookings

Jetstar is introducing live chat at Jetstar.com to offer customers a timely and convenient service to answer queries.

The live chat platform, which is available from today, allows Jetstar.com users to interact with customer service agents via an instant messaging interface on the website.

Jetstar Group Cheif Commercial Officer David Koczkar said the addition of this service was great news for customers.

"We know our customers value their time and our live chat service is all about resolving queries on the spot," Mr Koczkar said.

"Jetstar has always embraced the use of technology to improve the customer experience and we'er proud to be the first airline to offer live chat in Australia and New Zealand.

"This new platform helps us deliver a hassle-free experience and is another initiative we have implemented as part of our focus on continually improving the Jetstar customer experience."

Jetstar first used live chat in 2011 to help customers booking holiday packages on Jetstar.com and customer feedback for this service has been positive.

"Four out of five Jetstar customers who have used live chat have had their query resolved on first contact and customer satisfaction rates are around 90 per cent," Mr Koczkar added.

In July 2012, the live chat service was extended to include help for web users having trouble completing online bookings.

The software that supports Jetstar's live chat platform was developed by US technology firm LivePerson.

Live chat will only initially be available for Australian and New Zealand customers with other Jetstar markets currently under consideration.

About Jetstar

The Jetstar Group is one of Asia Pacific's fastest growing airline brands with one of the most extensive ranges of destinations in the region. It is made up of Jetstar Airways (subsidiary of the Qantas Group) in Australia and New Zealand, Jotstar Asia in Singapore, Jetstar Pacific in Vietnam, and Jetstar Japan in Japan, Jetstar branded carriers operate up to 4,200 flights a week to more than 75 destinations. The Jetstar Group carried more than 34 million passengers in financial year 2016.

Figure 7-5: Jetstar introduces web chat service.[6]
Reprinted with permission from Jetstar.

A typical live chat function has two text windows—one for customers to type their messages and the second box that displays service agents' responses. The result is a powerful and effective means of communication that helps to create an excellent service experience.[5]

Similar to phone calls, customers who choose to contact service agents via live chats are placed in a virtual queue and available service agents will get back to them in real time. This mode of communication can be useful for those who are not fluent in English or have problems understanding a particular accent.

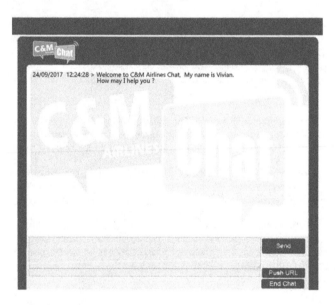

Figure 7-6: Live chat function.

Social media

Social media platforms can be easily accessed via computers and telecommunication devices such as tablets and mobile phones. This is becoming an increasing important communication channel as some of the younger tech-savvy customers prefer to interact with the airline via social media platforms. As such, more airlines are now dedicating service agents to handle enquiries and concerns to such channels of communication.

However, airline companies should be aware that social media platforms are different from other channels of communication as all

Figure 7-7: Thai Airways' social media platform on Twitter.
The above screenshot is reprinted with permission from Twitter.

content posted online can be read and shared by the public. Hence, service agents need to take particular care in ensuring that their replies are clear, concise, grammatically sound and are free from spelling errors when replying to these comments.

In cases whereby a particular concern or complaint raised on social media platforms is one that is best solved or discussed in private, it is recommended that service agents provide a general reply to acknowledge the comment before sending a customer involved a private message to follow up on the matter.

Email

Email is another channel for ease of communication between an airline and its customers. Similar to live chats and social media, emails can be easily sent anywhere and anytime, as long as one has access to the Internet and a computer device. Unlike the nature of social media platforms' comments, emails are private messages and only designate service agents who are in charge of the respective email accounts are able to access these contents. Upon receiving an email, airline service agents need to read the message before addressing the request or concern. Responding to an email is similar to writing a letter and formal business language should be used. It is important to use an appropriate subject line that clearly states the purpose of the email. Service agents must also ensure the message in the email is clear, precise and straight to the point. Last but not least, service agents need to check for grammar and spelling mistakes before sending out the email. It is always a good practice to read the drafted reply again before sending it out.

> Air Berlin Flight 8109 took off on August 9, 2013 without a single piece of checked baggage. To make matters even worse, it failed to locate any of the 200 passengers' missing baggage for weeks, causing a storm of Twitter complaints and a Facebook page devoted to the debacle.[7]

Figure 7-8: Sample email response.

COMMON WRITING MISTAKES

Below is a list of common mistakes made by service agents when drafting email responses. It is recommended for service agents who handle customers' queries and concerns via emails, live chats and social media platforms to take note of these in their responses as using the incorrect words will distort the original intention of the message.

Word	Definition	Example (what the message means)
Accept vs. Except		
Accept	(verb)—to receive or to take something that is offered	Please accept our sincere apologies. (We are sorry for what we have done.)
Except	(preposition)—not including someone or something	Alcohol is offered to all guests except customers under the age of 18 years old. (Customer under 18 years old will not be served alcohols. /We accept all kinds of credit cards except JCB.)
Advice vs. Advise		
Advice	(*noun*)—an opinion or suggestion about what someone should do	My advice is to contact your travel agent. (The travel agent will be able to tell you what the best options are.)
Advise	(*verb*)—to recommend or suggest something	I advise you to buy this product in white as I think it suits your skin color. (The cabin crew is telling the customer what is most suitable for her.)
Affect vs. Effect		
Affect	(*verb*)—to influence; to act on something and cause a change	I hope this incident will not affect our relationship. (I hope that this problem will not damage our relationship.)
Effect	(*noun*)—a change that results when something is done or happens: an event, condition, or state of affairs that is produced by a cause	The thunderstorm had an effect on the flight schedule. (The bad weather has caused many flight delays.)
Their vs. There vs. They're		
Their	(*adjective*)—relating to or belonging to certain people, animals or things	Their baggage is overweight. (These customers' baggage are overweight)
There	(*adverb*)—in that place; at that location	Please place your baggage over there. (Please put your baggage in that location.)
They're	contraction of "they are"	They're travelling to San Francisco. (This group of people is going to San Francisco.)
To vs. Too		
To	(*preposition*)—used to indicate the place, person or thing that someone or something moves toward	Would you like to proceed to the business lounge before boarding? (Before boarding, you can go to the business lounge if you'd like to.)

(Continued)

Word	Definition	Example (what the message means)
Too	*(adverb)*—also; in addition/more than what is wanted, needed, acceptable, possible, etc.	Can I have one too? (Can I also have one?)/ The weather is too cold. (It is colder than what I would have liked.)

Your vs. You're

Word	Definition	Example (what the message means)
Your	*(adjective)*—relating to or belonging to you	Is this your baggage? (Does this baggage belong to you?) May I have your signature? (Please sign over here.)
You're	contraction of "you are"	You're welcome. (You are welcome.)

Insure vs. Ensure vs. Assure

Word	Definition	Example (what the message means)
Insure	*(verb)*—to buy insurance for something	This policy will insure your travel against delays and baggage loss. (This policy will cover any losses due to delay of baggage or irregularity during travel.)
Ensure	*(verb)*—to guarantee; to make something sure, certain or safe	We ensure that you will be able to catch the connecting flight. (We guarantee that you will make it for the next leg of your flight.)
Assure	*(verb)*—to tell someone in a very strong and definite way that something will happen or that something is true	We assure you that your grandfather will be well taken care of during the flight. (We promised that we will take care of your grandfather throughout the duration of the flight.)

Its vs. It's

Word	Definition	Example (what the message means)
Its	*(adjective)*—to show ownership; possessive form of "it"	The baggage arrived with its contents damaged. (The baggage has arrived. However, the contents inside are damaged.)
It's	contraction of "it is/it has"	The flight cannot depart as it's started to snow. (The plane cannot depart as it is starting to snow.)

Whether vs. Weather

Word	Definition	Example (what the message means)
Whether	*(conjunction)*—used to indicate choices or possibilities from the plane or not.)	A captain makes the decision as to whether the passengers should stay on the aircraft. (A captain makes the decision on whether passengers should disembark.)
Weather	*(noun)*—the temperature and other outside conditions (such as rain, cloudiness, etc.) at a particular time and place	The weather is great and the flight will depart on time. (The conditions are good for taking off and the flight will depart on time.)

SUMMARY

The airline customer contact center is a department that handles customers' enquiries and complaints. It is a direct point where the airline service agents interact with customers. Customers can choose from a variety of communication channels to contact the contact center. These include telephone, emails, live chats and social media platforms. As these airline service agents' interactions with customers are limited to verbal and written forms of communication, they must be equipped with excellent listening, speaking and writing skills.

APPLYING THE KNOWLEDGE

True or false?

Are the following statements true or false? Put a tick in the right column.

Statement	True	False
1. The airline customer contact center serves as the secondary contact point between an airline and its customers.		
2. Airlines use an automatic call distribution system to segregate customers' incoming calls.		
3. Many airlines have added a real-time chat function in their website.		
4. The majority of customers expect a response to their voice messages within an hour.		
5. Service agents based in an airline contact center only require verbal skills when communicating with customers.		
6. Customers can sense service agents' attitudes by the tone of their voice.		
7. Service agents can hang up the phone immediately after successfully resolving customers' issues.		
8. Social media is becoming an important means of communication between an airline and its customers.		
9. Traditional mail is taking over email as a means of written communication.		
10. It is good practice to proofread an email response before it is sent out to the recipient.		

Multiple choice questions

Read the following questions and circle the correct answers.

1. When a customer asks for a discount, how should a service agent respond?
   a. "My apologies, I am unable to lower the price of your flight."
   b. "How can I do that? You should not bargain with me."
   c. "Your ticket is already very cheap. I cannot further lower the price."
   d. "I'd suggest for you to fly with another airline if you are looking for a cheaper flight."

2. How should a service agent respond when a customer is upset about a flight delay?
   a. "The flight has only been delayed for an hour. There is no need for you to be upset."
   b. "There is nothing I can do about this."
   c. "I would like to apologize on behalf of my company for this delay."
   d. "Do not blame us, blame the weather!"

3. How should a service agent respond when a customer asks a question that he or she does not know the answer to?
   a. "I don't know. Please ask someone else."
   b. "I am sorry but I am not sure."
   c. "I am sorry. I am not sure but I will find out and get back to you."
   d. "Can you please hold on the line? I will transfer you to another agent who might know the answer."

4. How should a service agent respond when a customer complains about the long waiting time on the phone?
   a. "I am sorry to keep you waiting."
   b. "You're lucky today. You'd have to wait longer if you had called yesterday."
   c. "What's your problem?"
   d. "You should call during the non-peak hours if you don't like waiting."

5. What should a service agent say at the end of a conversation with a customer?
   a. "You're welcome."
   b. "That's it!"

    c. "Can you please hang up first?"

    d. "Thank you for calling. Have a nice day and we hope to serve you again."

Short-answer questions

Imagine you are conducting a training course for service agents. You have been given a list of common mistakes made by some of these agents. Rewrite the following questions and sentences in the most appropriate manner.

1. Who are you?
2. What do you want?
3. What is your name?
4. You can only pay by cash or credit card.
5. I don't understand what you are talking about?
6. Say it again.
7. We cannot give you a discount.
8. Please speak louder.
9. Our airline does not have any direct flights to Bangkok. You can contact another airline.
10. We don't serve free meals on board this flight. You need to purchase your meals from the cabin crew if you are hungry.

Circle the correct answer

Read the conversation and circle the most appropriate answers.

Service agent:	Good morning and welcome to C&M Airline, my name is Joseph. (1) What do you want?/How can I help you today?/Who are you looking for?
Customer:	Hi. I would like to make a reservation for a flight from Manila to Hong Kong.
Service agent:	Certainly, may I have your last name, please?
Customer:	Yoshiba
Service agent:	Mr. Yoshiba, when would you like to depart from Manila?

Customer:	This Sunday, please.
Service agent:	Sure. Mr. Yoshiba, you have requested for a flight for this Sunday, 21 August. We have a morning flight and an afternoon flight. (2) Which one do you want?/What flight do you want?/Which one do you prefer?
Customer:	I'd like the morning flight, please.
Service agent:	Would you like to travel by business class or economy class?
Customer:	Economy class.
Service agent:	Certainly, (3) What is/May I have/Tell me your full name, please?
Customer:	Takahashi Yoshiba.
Service agent:	Could I trouble to spell out your full name, please?
Customer:	My first name is T-A-K-A-H-A-S-H-I and my last name is Y-O S-H-I-B-A.
Service agent:	Mr. Yoshiba, (4) Would you also like/Do you want/Don't you want to book a return flight?
Customer:	It's okay. I would like a one-way flight.
Service agent:	Sure. (5) What is/Tell me/May I have your contact number, please?
Customer:	It is 7475643937.
Service agent:	Mr. Yoshiba, your booking on 21 August has been confirmed. The flight number is CM 2234. The departure time from Manila is 0900 hr and the arrival time at Hong Kong 1030 hr.
Service agent:	Mr. Yoshiba, the total cost of the air ticket, including taxes is 30,000 peso. (6) You must/Would you like to/Don't you want to pay by debit card or credit card?
Customer:	I would like to pay by credit card, via Visa payment please. Here are my credit card details. 4587-4757-8474-3738. The expiry date is August 2020.
Service agent:	Thank you, Mr. Yoshiba. Your booking is now confirmed. Would you like to have the reference number?
Customer:	Yes, please.

Service agent: It is "A" for Africa, number 3, number 7, "R" for Russia, "S" for Switzerland and "N" for Netherlands. Please remember to arrive at the airport three hours before departure on 21 August for check-in.

Customer: Sure.

Service agent: Are there anything else (7) You want today?/I can help with today?/You demanded today?

Customer: No, that's all.

ENDNOTES

1. Borowski, C. (2014, May 27). You Need to Offer Callback—Here Are 3 Ways to Get It. Software Advice: http://hello-operator.softwareadvice.com/3-ways-to-offer-callback-0514/

2. For Dummies. (2015). Improving Your Inflection on the Phone. John Wiley & Son: http://www.dummies.com/how-to/content/improving-your-inflection-on-the-phone.html

3. The National Center for Voice and Speech. (2015). Voice Qualities. The National Center for Voice and Speech: http://www.ncvs.org/ncvs/tutorials/voiceprod/tutorial/quality.html

4. ISV Kaizen. (2007). Address your customer by their names. ISV Kaizen: http://www.drexplain.com/isv-kaizen-blog/support/address-your-customer-by-their-names/

5. Shelton, A. (2015). Customer service training: using live chat for customer service. Customer service skills: http://www.customerserviceskills.net/customer_service_skills_Using-Live-Chat-for-Customer-Service.htm

6. Jetstar. (2013). Jetstar introduces web chat service for customers.: http://newsroom.jetstar.com/jetstar-introduces-web-chat-service-for-customers/

7. Annis, R. (2013 Sep 5). Airlines Can't Keep Up With Customers' Social Media Complaints. Gadling: http://gadling.com/2013/09/05/airlines-social-media-complaints/

CHAPTER EIGHT

Customer Service at the Airport

Chapter Outline

Learning Objectives

After reading this chapter, the reader should be able to:

- Understand the customer service at airport
- Recognize an airline's internal and external customers
- Make the necessary preparations prior to opening of check-in counters
- Identify types of interaction between service agents and customers at various locations within the airport terminal

CUSTOMER SERVICE AT THE AIRPORT

At the airport, frontline service agents are positioned at various locations to offer assistance to customers. These service agents are also known as customer service representatives (CSR) or ground service agents (GSA). Some airlines have outsourced parts of these services to external companies and these agents are known as ground handling agents (GHA). At the airport, these frontline service agents interact with customers and provide services such as issuing boarding pass and checking in baggage. Their scope of work extends to interacting with customers at various airport facilities, boarding and disembarking of aircraft, providing arrival service and baggage services. Airport ground agents interact with internal and external customers in their day-to-day duties.

Internal customers
- Airline staff
  - Agents from other departments such as the customer contact center enquiring about customer reservation related matters pertaining to airfares and flight schedules.
  - Check-in airline staff traveling on standby status.
- Other airline staff
  - Organize customers transiting from the company's airline to another airline due to irregular operations.
  - Check status of transfer baggage from one airline to another.
- Other partners
  - Ramp agents inquire about baggage delivery status
  - Catering agents take care of issues related of loading of carts
  - Cleaning staff in charge of lost and found items and cleaning status of aircraft for turnaround flights

External customers
- Airline customers
  - Check in customers, issue boarding pass and baggage tags
  - Offer service in the airline lounge
  - Assist customers in boarding aircraft

○   Assist arrival customers
○   Offer assistance in retrieving customers' checked baggage.

FIRST IMPRESSIONS

First impressions are created during the initial contact between frontline service agents and customers. This is important for airlines as customers often judge the quality of an airline and the professionalism of its agents based on the first impression. A customer is able to evaluate the level of quality provided by service agents and form an opinion about them based upon their appearances, body language, behavior, gestures, and grooming within the first three seconds of an interaction.[1]

To ensure a minimum standard of service, airlines have set the following basic guidelines for service agents:

- Prepare ahead of time
- Be punctual
- Maintain a professional appearance
- Ensure tidiness of check-in counters

PREPARING AHEAD OF TIME

Before the check-in counter opens, agents who are on duty need to attend a pre-shift briefing session that addresses all operational matters and information about passengers who are traveling on a particular day. It is crucial to be well-informed about all passengers, especially those who need extra assistance. Being familiar and up-to-date on the industry's latest happenings and current events help service agents to be more knowledgeable and well-prepared for their duties, hence creating a positive impression.

Be punctual
Ensure that check-in counters are opened at the official stated time. Most airlines today recommend customers to check in at least 3 hours before

departure. In return, customers expect agents to be ready to help them check in upon arrival at the airport.

Professional appearance

As customers tend to judge service agents' ability and knowledge based on their appearance, this has a direct impact on the confidence and level

Figure 8-1: Service agents' personalities are demonstrated by their appearance.

of trust that they have in an airline. Customers often approach agents who are friendly and neat in appearance as these are first impression "signs" an agent will be willing to assist them and solve their problems as compared to another agent who looks tired and shows signs of boredom.

Airlines and ground handling companies have established strict attire and appearance policies that require all frontline service agents to wear standard uniforms and female agents to put on makeup while on duty. The purpose of such appearance policies is to reinforce an airline's overall image of helpfulness and readiness to serve customers.

Tidiness of check-in counter and waiting time

The check-in counter also plays an important part in creating a positive first impression. Customers usually evaluate a check-in counter's setup while waiting to check in. A messy counter setup gives customers the impression that an airline is disorganized and not well prepared to serve its customers.

A good counter setup includes a standard queuing system where customers can wait in line to check in. In addition, the neatness of the queue and the duration of the waiting time have an influence on the perceived professionalism of an airline. Customers tend to have high expectations with regard to check-in time and can become impatient very quickly in an open-queue scenario whereby there are different queues for them to choose from. If they choose a line that is moving slower than the adjacent lines; dissatisfaction is created. Some airlines now use the common queue system, also known as the bank queue system in order to eliminate this problem. This system of having customers to line up in a single queue which is served by multiple check-in counters helps to reduce overall waiting time.

To segregate the different types of customers, airlines set up designated counters for first class and business class travelers, and those who are enrolled in frequent-flier programs. This helps airlines to ensure that their premium customers who have higher expectations are taken care of soonest.

FACE-TO-FACE INTERACTIONS

At the counter

Airline ground agents spend the majority of their time interacting with customers at the check-in counters. The roles of these agents are to verify customers' travel documents, assign them to their seats, confirm any special service request and accept customers' baggage. This entire check-in process usually lasts between 5 and 10 minutes, during which ground service agents use the airline's departure management system to issue boarding passes and baggage tags to customers.

Greetings

When customers approach the check-in counter, service agents may initiate the interaction with a formal greeting. This usually includes some polite words that demonstrate welcomeness. A formal greeting can begin with a simple greeting that indicates the time of the day. This is then followed by the main greeting message that includes a salutation based on the customer's gender and a personalized message that asks about his or her well-being as seen in the example below:

Time of the day greeting		Customer's gender	Greeting message
Good morning	00:00 to 11:59	(Male) sir,	how are you doing?
Good afternoon	12:00 to 17:59	(Female) madam,	what can I do for you?
Good evening	18:00 to 23:59		where is your destination today?

Checking in

To complete the check-in process, service agents need to obtain some basic information such as travel documents and flight details from customers.

Figure 8-2: Flow of check-in process.

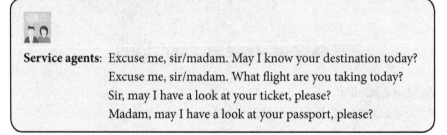

Service agents: Excuse me, sir/madam. May I know your destination today?
Excuse me, sir/madam. What flight are you taking today?
Sir, may I have a look at your ticket, please?
Madam, may I have a look at your passport, please?

As soon as agents obtain customers' travel documents, they will need to identify and address them using the correct salutation (i.e. Mr. or Miss.) followed by their last name as this demonstrates personalized service.

Breaking the ice

While checking in customers, service agents may choose to engage in some small talk. Ice-breaking helps to create a relaxing and comfortable environment, and strengthens the relationship between an airline and its customers. This also makes customers feel at ease, especially for those who are flying for the first time or nervous about taking flights. Ways to initiate a conversation include asking some simple questions, making a general comment, or stating some opinions and facts.[2]

One of the best ways to break the ice is to ask some simple and general questions in order to kick-start the conversation. Below are some useful topics and phrases:

Topics	Phrases
Weather	It is so hot today, isn't it? Wow! It's really windy today.
Trip	How was your trip? Did you visit the Grand Palace during your stay? (for tourists departing from Bangkok's Suvarnabhumi Airport)
Casual comments	I really like the color of your luggage. Where did you get it? You have a very nice-looking pair of earrings. (only appropriate for female service agents)

Based on customers' response, service agents can further extend the conversation dialogue to express care. This can be done by identifying their purpose of travel and bringing up various topics that might be of interest to them.

Customers' purpose of travel can usually be identified by their appearance, belongings and the passport they are holding. Leisure travelers tend to wear casual clothing. They also usually travel in groups and have plenty of baggage. Business travelers on the other hand, tend to wear formal clothing, travel solo and have limited baggage.

Outbound and inbound customers can also be easily identified by their travel documents. Customers traveling outbound often use their originating country's travel documents while those returning home use the destination country's passport. For example, an agent in Malaysia checks in a couple with their newborn infant. The family has checked in two full luggage bags and is traveling to India with Malaysian passports. These are "clues" that these customers are traveling to India for leisure. On the other hand, an agent who checks in a customer bound for Phnom Penh International Airport, holding a Cambodian passport and wearing a suit at Shanghai Pudong International Airport is very likely returning home after a business trip.

Once agents identify a customer's purpose of travel and whether they are inbound or outbound travelers, they can use different dialogues to engage in a conversation with the customer while they sort out the boarding pass. Being too focused and ignoring customers whilst processing their documents may convey a negative impression. Below are some topics related to holiday experience, culture and food for leisure travelers, and casual questions pertaining to purpose of travel, duration of stay and flight experience for business travelers.

Leisure travelers (Outbound)	Business travelers (Outbound)
Are you going to Ho Chi Minh City for a vacation with your family members?	Will you be going to China after your meeting in Hong Kong?
How many days will you be staying in Singapore?	How many days will you be traveling?
I heard that the weather is quite warm in Malaysia at this time of the year!	How do you find our new business-class seats?
Leisure travelers (Inbound)	**Business travelers (Inbound)**
How was your trip? Did you have fun in Bangkok?	How was your business trip in Bangkok?
Have you tried the famous Tom Yam Kung? (food)	How long was your trip?
Have you been to the Grand Palace? (tourist attraction)	When will you be back again?

 Caution

Not all customers like socializing. If a customer chooses not to respond or is uncomfortable doing so, it is recommended for agents to simply focus on the check-in process so as to avoid disservice.

After issuing the boarding pass, service agents need to ask customers about the number of baggage they would like to check in. They can also ask additional questions to ensure that all no prohibited items have been checked in.

Mrs. Wang, How many luggage bags would you like to check in today?
Do you have any bags to check in?
May I inspect the items inside your baggage?
Could you please advise what this item is?

Recap

After the check-in process is completed and the baggage taken care of, agents should inform customers what has been done. This is also known as a recap. Information that needs to be conveyed to customers include details on the boarding pass such as departure time, boarding time and boarding gate's location so as to ensure customers do not miss their flights. Agents should also check the baggage receipt to confirm the number of checked-in baggage and the destination. It is also sometimes necessary to provide additional directions to the boarding gate, especially for first-time travelers who are not familiar with the air travel process.

Service agents: Mrs. Korwa, please proceed this way and you will see the security checkpoint after passing immigrations. Please follow the "A2" sign and you will reach the boarding gate. As the security checkpoint is congested due to the high travel season, please proceed through the security and immigration as early as possible. Thank you.

Recap of boarding pass information

Service agents: Mrs. Korwa, here is your boarding pass from Kuala Lumpur to Chiang Mai on flight CM886. The flight will be departing from gate A2 at 11:00 pm. Boarding will begin at 10:15 pm. Please be at the gate before that. You have been assigned to 35H, which is an aisle seat at 35H. In addition, here is your baggage receipt. You also have two check-in luggage bags. Thank you.

Thank the customers

The check-in process will be completed after service agents thank customers for their business. A sincere "thank you" also demonstrates gratitude and can make customers feel they are valued. According to research conducted by Harvard Business School's Associate Professor Francesca Gino, receiving expressions of gratitude makes a person feel a heightened sense of self-worth and that in turn, triggers other helpful behaviors toward customers.[3]

Sample:

> **Mr. Orchid,** Thank you very much for choosing to fly with us today. Thank you for flying with us. We wish you a great flight! Thank you for your business and have a great day.

AIRPORT SERVICE AGENTS' BEHAVIOR

Customers expect the check-in process to start as arrive at the check-in counter, and will form a negative impression of an airline if service agents are not available to attend to their needs. According to the article 'The Psychology of Waiting Lines' written by David Maister, an expert on business management practices and the management of professional service firms, customers often feel like they're waiting longer than they actually are, especially when they see that service agents are not

Figure 8-3: An example of unacceptable service agent behavior.

performing their duties efficiently.[4] These behaviors include chatting and jostling around with colleagues, leaving their workstations frequently and not attending to customers. This is similar to that of a supermarket with multiple cashiers. If one queue is moving relatively slower the others, customers will have the tendency to switch to other queues.

> ### Going the extra mile
> An elderly customer did not request for any seats when he made reservations for his flight. During check-in, he was assigned a middle seat on the airplane. He tried to change his seat but was unable to do so as the flight was full. While waiting to board the flight, a service agent called out for him over the intercom and when he approached the podium, he was informed that he has been assigned an aisle seat. The customer was pleased that the service agents taken the necessary actions to fulfill his requests.

At the lounge
Service agents are usually stationed at the first-class or business-class lounges where premium customers are invited to relax while waiting to board their flights. The main duties of these service agents are to verify the eligibility of customers who have access to the lounge area by checking their boarding pass and offering assistance whenever possible.

>
>
> **Service agent**: Good morning, madam. Welcome to the business class lounge. May I see your boarding pass, please?
>
> *The agent then verifies the customer's membership status by scanning her boarding pass.*
>
> **Service agent**: Mrs. Yokohama, thank you very much. Could you please follow me to the lounge? Please note that boarding announcements will be made when your flight is ready for boarding.

On occasions whereby a passenger does not have access to the first-class or business-class lounge:

Service agent: Mrs. Yokohama, I am sorry to inform you that the lounge is reserved for business class and gold card members. Would you like to purchase a one-time access pass?

Lounge service agents stationed inside the lounge are also responsible for informing passengers about the status of their flights. Airline lounges are often located away from the main boarding gate area, service agents will need to ask these passengers to proceed to the boarding gate in advance as the majority of them are entitled to priority boarding. Service agents also need to make announcements such as the one below through a separate announcement system. On other occasions, announcements are made specifically within the lounge area to update customers on their flight status.

Service agents: Ladies and gentlemen, may I have your attention please? Due to some mechanical problems, flight CM423 will be delayed. All customers taking this flight are encouraged to remain in the lounge area and wait for further information. C&M Airline apologizes for the inconvenience caused. Thank you.

Boarding gate

Service agents stationed at the boarding gate have very limited interactions with customers. These include assisting customers to board the aircraft, and offering additional services to customers who may require special assistance. These service agents' primary goal is to maintain the standard of service at the boarding gate areas.

These days, many airlines offer pre-boarding services that allow customers who have special needs to board the aircraft first. These customers include passengers in wheelchairs, those who travel with young children, pregnant women and children below the age of 12 who travel alone. Pre-boarding allows service agents to focus on passengers who may require more assistance and attention by assisting them with their carry-on baggage or helping them across the jet bridge. However, service agents are advised against carrying infants on behalf of the customers as there may be a risk of accidents.

Before the actual boarding begins, service agents will announce the boarding process. First-class and business-class customers generally board the plane before economy-class customers. This is part of the privilege of customers who paying more for their airfare. Allowing premium customers to settle down before others board the plane also ensures they have sufficient space to store their carry-on baggage.

Priority boarding, in particular, is increasingly common because commercial flights are usually full, and overhead bin space often fills up before all of the remaining non-priority customers board the airplane. These customers are then required to hand over their carry-on bags, which are whisked away to be "gate-checked", and more often than not, these passengers do not have time to retrieve the reading material or electronic devices they have brought along for the flight.[5]

Public announcements

The purpose of public announcements is to update on flight status and inform passengers to board their flights. The structure of the public announcement includes a greeting, a main message and ends with an acknowledgment.

Figure 8-4: Public announcement message structure.

During general boarding, service agents collect customers' boarding pass and inspect their travel documents to ensure they are on the correct flight. When inspecting passengers' boarding pass and travel documents, service agent should pay attention to their names as much as possible, make eye contact and address them by their last names as they enter the boarding gate. This also serves as the last round of safety "check" for any intruders.

Figure 8-5: Sequence of public announcement.

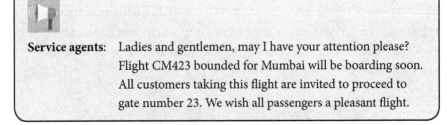

Service agents: Ladies and gentlemen, may I have your attention please? Flight CM423 bounded for Mumbai will be boarding soon. All customers taking this flight are invited to proceed to gate number 23. We wish all passengers a pleasant flight.

While public announcements have minimal effect on customer satisfaction, one that is made with the appropriate tone and voice demonstrates the professionalism.

Figure 8-6: Service agent making a public announcement.

> **Thank you, Ms. Wang.** We wish you a nice/wonderful/great flight
> We hope you will enjoy your flight.
> Have a pleasant flight.

The little things that make a big difference

While boarding a flight bounded for Tokyo, a frantic customer called out to the cabin crew and informed her that he had left a camera at the security checkpoint. As the flight was about to take off, the passenger was worried as he would have to depart without his camera and end up losing it. The cabin crew quickly informed the ground service agent. As the security checkpoint was located quite a distance away from the boarding gate, they were unable to deliver the camera in time. The cabin crew calmed the customer down whilst ground service agents noted the customer's flight details. As the customer had to catch a connecting flight at Tokyo's Narita International Airport before reaching his final destination at San Francisco, the ground service agent asked him to contact the local service agent upon arrival at San Francisco International Airport. When the passenger arrived at San Francisco International Airport, he was surprised to see a service agent with his camera. This unfortunate incident became a memorable experience for the customer and he eventually became a frequent flyer of the airline.

Arrival

Upon arrival at the airport, there are service agents stationed at the terminal building to offer assistance to passengers who either need to transfer to another flight or have arrived at their destination. Passengers who are traveling for the first time and are new to the airport environment will rely on service agents to give them accurate directions and information. Service agents stationed here need to pay attention to disembarking passengers and proactively offer help to the elderly, customers traveling with small children, pregnant women, and those who need additional assistance.

Figure 8-7: Service agent paging a customer upon arrival.

Service agent: May I assist you with your carry-on bag?
Do you have a connecting flight? Do you have an onward boarding pass?
Please collect your baggage at belt number 11.

During irregular operations whereby an aircraft's arrival time is delayed, passengers rely on service agents to provide the necessary information and to make arrangements for their new connecting flight. Some customers may be worried or frustrated as their itinerary has been affected due to the delay. As such, service agents should understand these customers' feelings and offer help whenever possible.

Service agents also have the option of singling out a particular customer who needs assistance via paging. A paging sign lists the customer's information and helps service agents to identify him or her. Paging signs usually include the following information: connecting flight number or other detailed such as mishandled baggage. Informing affected customers about the bad news in advance demonstrates an airline's proactiveness in helping customers to resolve their problems.

Service Agent: Mrs. Shee, your connecting flight is departing soon. Please follow me to the boarding gate for your connecting flight. Mr. Zhen, I am sorry to inform you that one of your baggage was not loaded onto the flight. Please contact our baggage staff at the baggage area. They will assist you on filing the baggage mishandling report.

Baggage service

The baggage counter or office is manned by service agents, and the majority of customers who interact with these service agents do so because of baggage related problems.

Many airlines also station service agents at the baggage belt to offer immediate help to customers who have problems retrieving their baggage. Some customers may forget the type and color of their checked baggage after a long-haul flight. Agents stationed at the baggage belt area help these customers to identify and retrieve their baggage. These service agents usually keep a lookout for customers who have waited for an extended period of time at the baggage belt area. Having such service agents demonstrates an airline's sense of responsibility, and care and concern for its customers.

Service agent: Excuse me, sir. Are you still waiting for your baggage?
Customer: Yes, I am.
Service agent: Can I please see your baggage claim check? In addition, what is the color of your baggage?
Customer: Sure, here you go. It is brown color.
Service agent: Oh! Is that baggage over there yours?
Customer: Oh yes, it's that one. I must be too tired after the 13-hour flight! Thank you so much for your help!

At the baggage hall

It is normal for customers who are unable to find their baggage to show frustration when they approach service agents stationed at the baggage hall. Service agents responsible for this area should be patient and show care and concern even though it is the airline's fault for failing to deliver customers' baggage.

Figure 8-8: An angry customer at the baggage hall.

Service agents must apologize to these customers on behalf of the airline and assist them to resolve the problem by helping them to complete the property irregular report and keep them posted on the baggage delivery process. Even though many customers often ask for the exact date and time they can expect their baggage to arrive, service agents must not make any promises in an attempt to pacify them. These customers are already disappointed with the delayed baggage and if they do not receive their baggage as per what service agents have promised, the airline's reputation will be tarnished.

Service agents stationed at the baggage counter or office are responsible for following up on customers' delayed baggage. These service agents should endeavor to contact these customers with the latest information, and to reassure them at least once a day that the airline is working on sorting out their baggage in instances whereby there is no updated information available. In addition, they should only call customers during office hours (0830 to 1700), unless special instructions have been given.

Service agent: Please accept our apologies, Mr. Torres. We will deliver the baggage to you as soon as it arrives.

Customer: What time would that be?

Service agent: Unfortunately, I am unable to confirm the exact time. However, I will be sure to contact you once our agent has loaded the baggage onto the next flight that will be departing from Taipei in 3 hours.

Customer: Sure. Please make sure you call me as soon as possible.

Service agent: Definitely, Mr. Torres.

Service agent: Good evening, can I speak to Mrs. Sakura please?

Customer: Yes, I am.

Service agent: Mrs. Sakura, this is Jonathan calling from C&M Airline with regard to your delayed baggage. I would like to inform you that your baggage is now en-route to Bangkok from Abu Dhabi. Our agent at Abu Dhabi airport has already confirmed that the baggage was loaded onto flight CM 422 which will arrive in Bangkok at approximately 5:25 pm today.

Customer: Great! Will I be able to get my baggage tonight?

Service agent: I'll call you again to confirm the delivery time once your baggage arrives at the airport. Once again, thank you for your kind understanding and we apologize for the inconvenience caused.

Two Successful Customer Service Case Studies from (Surprise!) the Airlines

By Ted Janusz[6]

Article reprinted with permission from Business 2 Community

How do you lose a piece of carry-on luggage? Delta did that to me today. It was gate checked on the commuter flight from Atlanta to Birmingham, then didn't show up on the ramp when I arrived. Those of us from the flight missing luggage asked at the American baggage claim office in Birmingham if there was a representative for Delta. (The little area for Delta's baggage claim office was dark and the door was locked.)

The rep for American just became defensive and hostile as he responded while walking away. Finally, the Delta baggage service representative showed up. Now as Jerry Seinfeld says, "Nobody announces 'I want to work in Baggage Service when I grow up.'" But this employee may have been the exception.

Allan Day has worked for Delta for 27 years, in various positions. He began his day today by first listening empathetically to our plights and quickly communicating that he was on our side. Allan then exhibited a sense of urgency to resolve the problem. Compared to the reception we received from the American rep, we couldn't help but feel better knowing that Allan was doing all that he could to locate our lost luggage.

In addition to giving me free frequent flyer points, Allan gave me food vouchers to use while I waited for my found piece to come in on the next flight—even another voucher to use tomorrow night.

"Judging from my experience, what probably happened was that your luggage went back to Atlanta. I sincerely apologize, but that is the most likely case. I'll post a bulletin in my system so that the employees there will be on the lookout for it, retrieve it and send it back."

Allan then wrote down his name and number and asked me to be sure to give him a call before the next flight from Atlanta arrived. What he described was exactly what happened.

Checking in with Allan later, he said, "Good news! I just checked with Atlanta. Your bag will be here on the 8:40 flight!"

I teach customer service but tonight, Allan Day taught me a few lessons. "I just treat the customer the way I know I would want to be treated if it happened to me," he explained.

(Somehow I get the feeling that if my encounter had instead been with the representative from America, he would have tried to make me feel bad for inconveniencing him and trying to ruin his day.)

If you are ever in Birmingham Airport, stop by Delta Baggage Service, smile and say 'Hi' to Allan Day!

United Airlines Delays Flight for Dying Mother[7]

Article reprinted with permission from Help Scout

It's always heart-wrenching when a close family member passes. Sharing the final moments with a person we love can be a small respite in a truly difficult situation.

When Kerry Drake got on his United Airline flight, the mother he was en-route to see was facing her final hours. To add an extra layer of distress, Drake knew that if he missed his connecting flight he would likely not see her before she passed.

After his first flight got delayed, Drake broke down into tears on the plane. The flight attendants soon noticed his state and quickly found out what was wrong. Within minutes, Drake's dilemma was relayed to the captain, who radioed ahead to Drake's next flight.

The flight's crew responded by delaying the flight's departure to make sure he got on board.

"I was still like maybe 20 yards away when I heard the gate agent say, 'Mr. Drake, we've been expecting you,'" he said.

When Drake finally sat on the second flight, he realized how much went into getting him onto the plane.

"I was overcome with emotion!"

The result of many agent members working together to go above-and-beyond the call of duty to help this customer was that Drake made it to the hospital in time to see his mother.

Drake wrote the agent a heartfelt "thank you" letter expressing his immense gratitude for a team who was willing to pull out all the stops to assist in any way they could.

"At one point she opened her eyes, and I think she recognized me," said Drake, who spent the night at the hospital. "Around 4 am, she had a real moment of coherence, a last rally, although we didn't know it at the time. It was the last time."

She died that very morning.

In the coverage of this story on CNN, consumer advocate Christopher Elliot said,

"Airline employees are evaluated based on their ability to keep a schedule. Airlines compete with each other on who has the best on-time departure record. When the crew on this flight heard about this distraught customer trying to make his connection, they must have said, 'To hell with it'... and they made the right call."

We think so, too.

SUMMARY

The majority of interactions between service agents and customer take place at the airport terminal. Prior to opening of check-in counters, service agents must make the necessary preparations so that they are ready to serve the customers. Service agents stationed at check-in counters, lounges, boarding gates and arrival halls offer assistance to passengers and ensure that have a hassle-free travel experience. Service agents must also act proactively to resolve customers' problem so as to increase their level of satisfaction.

APPLYING THE KNOWLEDGE

True or false?

Are the following statements true or false? Put a tick in the right column.

Statement	True	False
1. Ground service agents are positioned in the airport terminal building to offer assistance to customers.		
2. The service agent should greet customers "Good morning" at all times.		
3. Customers who travel in a group usually check in at the same counter.		
4. Service agents should wait for customers to speak first before starting a conversation.		
5. All interactions with customers at the check-in counter should always conclude with a recap of the flight details.		
6. The psychological waiting time often seems shorter than the actual waiting time.		
7. Public announcements have a much lesser impact on customer satisfaction in comparison to personal interactions with customers at the boarding gate.		
8. First impressions are only generated when service agents talk to customers.		
9. Briefings are important as they allow the service team to share information about flights and operations before the check-in counters open.		
10. It is not necessary to keep check-in counters clean and tidy.		

Multiple choice questions

Read the following questions and circle the correct answer.

1. How should a service agent respond when a customer demands for an aisle seat?

   a. "Please wait a moment. Let me check the availability and get back to you."

   b. "The flight is full. Sorry I can't help you."

   c. "Can you ask the passenger seated next to you whether he or she would like to swop seats?"

   d. "No, it's impossible. The flight is full."

2. How should a service agent respond when a customer requests for a flight upgrade?

   a. "You cannot ask for that."

   b. "No upgrade is available unless you pay for it."

   c. "We don't have an upgrade option."

   d. "Certainly, would you like to pay by cash or credit card?"

3. How should a service agent respond when a customer complains that another customer is cutting the queue?
   a. "Hey. You need to return to the back of the queue."
   b. "Excuse me, sir. The line starts at the back. Could you please join the queue from there?"
   c. "I am busy."
   d. "What do you mean? You can't cut the queue!"
4. How should a service agent respond when a customer arrives late at the boarding gate?
   a. "Do you know that you are late?"
   b. "Why are you late? Where have you been?"
   c. "My apologies. The flight has already departed."
   d. "Do you know what's the time now?"
5. How should a service agent respond when a customer demands for his/her delayed baggage?
   a. "It's too bad. You need to wait for it."
   b. "My apologies, I am unable to fulfill your request."
   c. "This is not my problem."
   d. "What do you expect me to do?"

Short-answer questions

1. How do customers judge an airline's service based on its service agents? Explain your answer in full sentences.
2. Write a list of internal and external customers that service agents interact with at the airport.
3. What are the various behaviors that customers take note of when observing service agents while they are waiting to be checked in? Explain your answer in full sentences.
4. You are a service agent station at the baggage hall. You have just been briefed by your supervision that some baggage have not been loaded onto the aircraft for a particular flight due to weight restrictions. Upon arrival of said flight, the owners of these baggage your counter to enquire about their belongings. What do you do? Explain your answer in full sentences.

ENDNOTES

1. Skillsyouneed. (2015). Personal appearance. Skillsyouneed: http://www.skillsyouneed.com/ps/personal-appearance.html

2. Jerome, G. (2015). How to Break the Ice and Meet New People. Reader's Digest: http://www.rd.com/advice/relationships/how-to-break-the-ice-and-meet-new-people/#ixzz3dr2HvsGC

3. Leddy, C. (2013, Mar 19). The power of 'thanks'. Havard Gazetter: http://news.harvard.edu/gazette/story/2013/03/the-power-of-thanks/

4. Maister, D. (1985). The Psychology of Waiting Lines. davidmaister.com: http://davidmaister.com/articles/the-psychology-of-waiting-lines/

5. Sharkey, J. (2012, Jan 12). Selling Boarding Perks to the Forlorn. The New York Times: http://www.nytimes.com/2012/01/17/business/looking-for-better-treatment-when-boarding-on-the-road.html?_r=1

6. Janusz, T. (2013, Dec 3). "Two Successful Customer Service Case Studies from (Surprise!) the Airlines." Business 2 Community: http://www.business2community.com/customer-experience/two-successful-customer-service-case-studies-surprise-airlines-0702586#ZgzUMBckXVAesdWR.99

7. Help Scout. (2016). "United Airlines Delays Flight for Dying Mother", Help Scout: http://www.helpscout.net/10-customer-service-stories/

CHAPTER NINE

In the Aircraft Cabin

Chapter Outline

Learning Objectives

After reading this chapter, the reader should be able to:
- Recognize the standard customer service required of cabin crew
- Recognize the importance of cabin crew's appearance
- Understand the importance of pre-flight preparation
- Identify different interactions between the cabin crew and customers

CUSTOMER SERVICE IN THE CABIN

The main duties of cabin crew are to ensure the safety and comfort of customers during the entire duration of a flight. Many airlines have strict rules pertaining to cabin crew's grooming and physical appearance so as to create a memorable flight experience for customers. Many airlines also use this as a branding strategy to promote airline's hospitality and services.

Once the aircraft door is closed for departure and the plane is ready for take-off, it is the responsibility of the cabin crew to take care of customers and ensure they enjoy their flight experience. Cabin crew's duties are to ensure the safety and comfort of all customers and it is mandatory for all crew to go through intensive safety and service trainings. These service trainings prepare cabin crew to handle different types of customer issues on a flight to minimize flight interruptions.

Appearance

Cabin crew's appearance plays a vital role in portraying an airline's image. The first impression of cabin crew is formed when they enter the airport passenger terminal and as soon as they board the aircraft. Cabin crew are dressed differently from ground agents and their uniform is specially designed to represent the airline as a brand. These uniforms are also made of natural and fabrics that are not easily combustible such as cotton and wool.

Personal grooming is equally important as the cabin crew is in direct contact with passengers. As such, it is essential for them to put on clean and neat uniform, have their hair tied up and their shoes polished so as to demonstrate professionalism. They must also maintain short and clean fingernails as they are required to handle food items during a flight.

An example is the iconic Singapore Girl that was first adopted by Singapore Airlines in 1972 and this became synonymous with the airline. The female cabin crew in their *sarong kebaya*-traditional blouse dress combination that originated from an ancient Javanese court, and is traditionally worn by women in Southeast Asia-came to represent the cabin crew's service, professionalism and essentially, airline's service quality.[1]

Pre-flight preparation

All cabin crew must attend a pre-flight briefing before a flight and one of the most important pieces of information is to go through during this briefing is customers' details. Reviewing all passengers' information data in advance allows the cabin crew to make preparations for different sorts of services that customers need. The information data include details of those who require special assistance, special requests and breakdown of passengers by nationality. Knowledge of customers' nationalities allows cabin crew to in the necessary preparations in advance. According to a survey conducted by Airline Passenger Experience Association, customers' behavior on-board can sometimes be predicted by their nationalities. For example, Australians have the tendency to consume more alcohol during a flight, Americans tend to work, British and Germans are chattier than passengers of other nationalities, and Chinese travelers are big fans of "sleeping, shopping and gaming."[2] As such, if a flight comprises mostly of Chinese customers, the cabin crew needs to ensure that the duty-free cart is replenished. On the other hand, it is a good idea to stock on a large volume of alcoholic beverages for a flight with Australian passengers. Being aware of the different nationalities also allows cabin crew to forecast the quantity of certain meals offered on-board a flight and they can plan in advance and update customers on the various meal options available.

Express Service

The majority of Chinese passengers expect immediate services. Chinese customers usually expect the cabin crew to offer the meal and beverage service as soon as an aircraft takes off. They also tend to finish their in-flight meals quickly and expect cabin crew to collect their meal trays as soon as possible.

Indian customers, especially those traveling by economy class, also expect speedy service. Cabin crew usually need to act fast when serving Indian customers beverages as they tend to finish their drinks quickly and are more likely to ask for a refill.

Delivering prompt service also prevents potential situations in which customers have to walk to the gallery to return their trays or to demand food and drinks, such as a recent incident which took place on a flight from Moscow to Hong Kong in 2015. The cabin crew was not quick enough to collect a customer's meal tray and the customer decided to leave it by the exit door instead.

THE IN-FLIGHT PROCESS

This includes boarding of aircraft, departure, en-route, arrival and disembarkation. During this process, the cabin crew's role is to deliver messages and services to the passengers on behalf of the airline.

Boarding

As soon as customers enter the aircraft cabin, there are cabin crew standing by at various locations to assist them. Cabin crew must be familiar with the aircraft layout and direct customers to their respective seats. Cabin crew stationed at the entry door are also known as greeters. Their duty is to welcome all customers on-board the aircraft. As greeters are the first people that customers interact with on the aircraft, it is important for them to create a pleasant and welcoming first impression. As customers enter the cabin, greeters will welcome the customers verbally.

Figure 9-1: A cabin crew greeting customers during boarding.

Cabin crew: Good morning, sir and welcome on-board. May I please have a look at your boarding pass?

Greeters then need to direct passengers to their seats after checking their boarding pass. This is especially important for wide-body aircrafts as passengers sometimes are confused about the seating arrangement and may take a longer time to find their seats. This will result in a congested aisle, which will then slow down the boarding process and may lead to flight delays.

First class and business class

These two premium classes carry a much smaller number of customers and cabin crew should memorize these customers' names in advance. When these customers have settled down in their seats, the cabin crew then needs to address them by their last name and introduce themselves.

To show hospitality, it is a standard to offer first and business-class customers a welcome drink. Cabin crew are usually occupied during the boarding process, and they can speed up the service time by asking customers to choose between two choices of beverages.

Cabin crew: Good afternoon, Mr. Maslow. Welcome on-board today's flight from Malaysia to New York. My name is Jenny. Please do not hesitate to contact me if you need anything. Would you like start with a glass of champagne or some orange juice?

General boarding
On a narrow-body aircraft

Cabin crew: Good morning, sir and welcome on-board. Seats ABC are on your right and HJK are on your left.

On a wide-body aircraft

Cabin crew: Good morning, sir and welcome on-board. Please turn right at the next aisle and you will find your seat.

Cabin crew are also on stationed at each section of the passenger cabin to assist customers to locate their seat and store their carry-on baggage in the overhead storage compartments.

Cabin crew: Good morning, sir. May I have your seat number?
Customer: 45A
Cabin crew: Your seat is by the window over there. You may store your carry-on baggage in the space above your seat or underneath the seat in front of you.

Seating problems
A full flight is due to take off. While boarding, a customer contacted a cabin crew and requested to sit next to her friend, who is seated two rows behind her assigned seat.

Scenario	Conversation	Explanation
Customer	I want to sit next to my friend.	–
Cabin crew	Where is your friend seating?	In order to understand the situation, the cabin crew asks for more information.
Customer	She is seated over there (pointing to a woman sitting two rows behind).	–
Cabin crew	Please take your seat first and I'll check if the seat next to your friend is available.	Do not reply immediately as this may demonstrate unhelpfulness.
Cabin crew	I am sorry, Madam. Our flight is completely full today and there are no empty seats available. I will check with the other passengers to see if I can make some arrangements.	Reply with an apology even though the cabin crew is not at fault. Cabin crew can also offer other options if they are unable to meet the customer's request.
Cabin crew	I am sorry, madam. I am unable to arrange for you to be seated next to your friend.	Reply with an apology.
Customer	Oh, never mind then.	–
Cabin crew	May I suggest for you to contact the reservation department to reserve your seats for future flights as that you will be able to sit with your traveling companions?	Provide recommendations and suggestions.
Customer	Sure, thank you.	–

PREPARING THE CABIN

After all passengers are on-board the aircraft, the cabin crew will secure the cabin and make the final preparations for departure. These include safety requirements such as ensuring customers are seated with their seat belt fastened and checking that all baggage are stored properly.

While the safety announcement is being made, cabin crew will perform a final thorough check through the passenger cabin to ensure all customers comply with the in-flight safety requests.

Cabin crew: Ladies and gentlemen, welcome on-board C&M Airline flight CM 3345 bounded for Chengdu, People Republic of China. In preparation for departure, please ensure that your seat belt is securely fastened and secure all baggage underneath your seat or in the overhead compartments. Please also make sure that your seats and table trays are stored in the upright position for takeoff. Please turn off all personal electronic devices, including laptops and mobile phones. Do note that smoking is strictly prohibited on this flight. Thank you for choosing C&M Airline. Enjoy your flight!

Cabin crew: Excuse me, sir. Please fasten your seat belt. Thank you. Excuse me, madam. Please place your handbag underneath the seat in front of you. Thank you. Excuse me, sir. As the plane is about to take off, please turn off your mobile phone. Thank you.

Safety demonstration

A safety demonstration is an informative presentation of the safety facilities on-board an aircraft and it must be shown prior to every flight departure. Some airlines broadcast a safety video via the in-flight entertainment system while members of the cabin crew perform a live demonstration in others. To ensure safety information is effectively communicated to customers, airlines are employing different strategies to attract their attention. Some airlines have taken a creative spin on their safety demonstrations and a number of these videos have even gone viral. Apart from getting the passengers' attention, this indirectly affects customer satisfaction as these interesting demonstrations form part of a passenger's air travel experience.

Airline	Form of safety demonstration	You Tube	YouTube links:
Southwest Airlines	Includes surprises and jokes in announcement		https://www.youtube.com/watch?t=62&v=07LFBydGjaM
Southwest Airlines	Rap		https://www.youtube.com/watch?v=DYA_ivyj3kE
Cebu Pacific	Dance		https://www.youtube.com/watch?v=aXY27Rwg6UQ
Virgin America	Dance and song		https://www.youtube.com/watch?v=r-eB-RPGezs
Bangkok Airways	Songs		https://www.youtube.com/watch?v=nc_-y56UiHM

In-flight announcement

Right after an aircraft has taken off, cabin crew will provide more information about the flight and the services available on-board. These are usually transmitted via announcements that are made via the cabin's public announcement system. In-flight announcements are made by the cabin crew at the crew station. All announcements have to be delivered at the right pace and in a clear voice as some customers are first-time flyers and are not familiar with in-flight announcements. Announcements should also not be made too slowly as the other customers might be bored.

Cabin crew: Ladies and gentlemen, once again, welcome on-board Flight CM 3345 to Chengdu. Our aircraft is under the command of Captain Narret and first officer, Champoom. The flight duration to Chengdu will be approximately four-and-a-half hours. Dinner will be served on today's flight and this will be followed by duty-free sales. A complimentary copy of our in-flight magazine can be found in the seat pocket in front of you. Please feel free to take this with you when you leave. We are glad to have you with us today. Please do not hesitate to let any of our cabin crew know if there is anything that we can do to make your journey more comfortable. We hope that you will enjoy your flight to Chengdu. Thank you.

In-flight service

Cabin crew begin offering in-flight services when the plane is airborne. These services include complimentary amenities such as beverages, meals, comfort kit and in-flight entertainment. Some low-cost airlines offering limited services and customers have to purchase additional amenities.

Airlines have adopted business strategies to attract the various types of customers. This can be seen in the differentiated services offered in full service and low-cost flights. For example, full service airlines adopt certain strategies that are different from low-cost airlines.

Beverages

Services differ in first-class and business class as compared to economy class. In first and business class, cabin crew will take orders for beverages from customers personally and prepare them in the galley before returning with their choice of drinks.

Cabin crew: Mrs. Chang, what would you like to drink?
Customer: Orange juice, please.
Cabin crew: Sure. Would you like it with or without ice?
Customer: Without ice, please.
Cabin crew: I'll be back in a minute.

On the other hand, cabin crew servicing passengers in the economy class use catering carts and prepare beverages in front of customers. As cabin crew are unable to memorize the name of every customer seated in the economy class due to the sheer volume of passengers, salutations are used to demonstrate courtesy.

Cabin crew: Good afternoon, sir. Would you like to have a drink?

On occasions whereby one or more items in the beverage cart are running low, cabin crew may sometimes limit customers' choices of beverages and only offer them the options that are still in stock as an open question allows customers to order from the entire range of beverages available.

Cabin crew: Good afternoon, sir. Would you like to have some water or a glass of apple juice?

Meal service

Meal services provide opportunities for cabin crew to interact with customers. Similar to beverages, meal services on first-class and business-class flights are served differently as compared to economy class. Each customer is given a menu and cabin crew will take their orders. Customers who have dietary restrictions may order their in-flight meals in advance. The cabin crew will then confirm these orders when the passengers have boarded the aircraft.

First and business class

It is important for the cabin crew to check with customers if they wish to be woken up for their meals as they can neither be kept for long after being heated nor reheated due to risk of food poisoning. Knowing customers' preference allows cabin crew to plan when they should heat up their meal so as to avoid any disservice. With the small number of passengers holding first and business-class tickets, cabin crew have time to interact with these customers. In addition, checking with customers if their meal is satisfactory shows care and concern.

Cabin crew:	Mr. Morreto, you have pre-ordered a vegetarian meal for today's flight. What drink would you like to have with your meal?
Customer:	I would like some apple juice, please.
Cabin crew:	Good afternoon, Mrs. Wang. What would you like to have for lunch today? For appetizer, we have a choice of smoked salmon with prawn or mango salad with chicken.
Customer:	Salmon, please.
Cabin crew:	How about the main course? We are serving shrimp mousse in red curry, pork schnitzel with mushroom sauce and beef with braised sauce.
Customer:	I'll take the shrimp.
Cabin crew:	Would you like to have any wine with your meal? For wine selections, we have Pouilly-Fumé from France, Chardonnay from California, Cabernet Sauvignon from France and Pinot Noir from Argentina.
Customer:	Water is fine. Thank you.
Cabin crew:	We will also be serving breakfast two hours prior to arrival at the destination. Would you like omelette with cheese, pork sausage with grill tomatoes or French toast with maple syrup?
Customer:	I'll take the omelette.
Cabin crew:	Sure. Could you please let us know if you are all right with us waking you up if you are asleep during meal service?
Customer:	Yes, please.
Cabin crew:	Thank you very much, Mrs. Wang.

On occasions, the cabin crew may ask customers in the premium class about their second choice of meal preference to avoid disturbing them during the flight.

Economy class

Cabin crew: Mr. Wang, we have a choice of shrimp mousse with red curry,
pork schnitzel with mushroom sauce and beef with braised
sauce.
Customer: I'd like shrimp mousse with red curry.
Cabin crew: Sure. And may I just check what would be your second choice
if we run out of shrimp during the meal service?
Customer: Ohh ... I'll have beef with braised sauce instead.
Cabin crew: Got it. Thank you very much, Mr. Johnson.

Special meals

Special meals are served first in the economy class. Unlike passengers in
first and business class, these customers do not get to choose from the
list available. However, cabin crew will confirm with customers who have
ordered a special meal. This practice allows cabin crew to ensure these
requested meals are delivered to the correct passengers.

A cabin crew approaches a passenger seated at row 32C.

Cabin crew: Mr. Park, I would like to confirm that you have ordered a low
sodium meal for this flight.
Customer: No, I didn't. I have just changed seats with that customer over
there.

Customer points at another passenger seated at row 34G.

Cabin crew: I see. Thank you, sir.

The cabin crew then approaches the passenger seated row 34G.

Cabin crew: Mr. Park, I would like to confirm that you have ordered a low
sodium meal for this flight.
Customer: Yes, I did. Thank you.

General meal

Cabin crew serve meals by pushing catering carts through the aircraft's aisles. It is a common practice to serve customers who are seated in the innermost seats followed by those sitting in the middle and finally, those seated by the aisle. This is to minimize incidents of toppling or spilling of food and drinks on other passengers. As most airlines do not offering menu to economy-class customers, it is the responsibility of the cabin crew to inform customers about the choices available. As cabin crew are serving more than one customer in the same row, they can choose to inform them about their meal choices either individually or all at the same time.

Cabin crew: Excuse me, sir. What would you like for lunch today? We have a choice of chicken with rice or pork with noodles.

Figure 9-2: A cabin crew offering meal service to economy-class passengers.

Airlines usually prepare in-flight meals according to statistics of the different meals that have been selected in prior flights and stock a larger quantity of the popular items. However, there is always a chance that the figures are underestimated. This then leads to a shortage of a particular choice of meal. When this happens, there are several communication strategies that the cabin crew can use to inform passengers.

Apologies

The simplest way is to apologize to customers and inform them that their choice of selection is no longer available and to check if they are all right with the other options. Most customers are understanding and will opt for what's available.

Cabin crew:	Excuse me, sir. We have chicken with rice and pork with noodles for today's lunch service. However, I am sorry to inform you that we have just run out of chicken rice. Do you mind taking the pork noodles instead? It just tastes as good as the chicken rice.

The story of a ham and cheese sandwich

On a thru flight from Boston to San Francisco via Denver, passengers were asked to stay on-board the flight at Denver while the remaining passengers disembarked and others boarded the connecting flight. A customer asked the cabin crew if he could purchase a ham and cheese sandwich. The cabin crew offered him some chocolate and chips instead as the pantry had run out of sandwiches. The customer refused and was very disappointed. A few minutes later, the cabin crew returned with a baked ham and cheese sandwich. The customer was pleasantly surprised as the cabin crew had gone out to the concourse to purchase the sandwich.

Making a choice more attractive

Cabin crew may sometimes choose to provide more details about a particular meal during meal service to encourage customers to have a preference of one meal over the other.

Cabin crew: Excuse me, sir. For today's lunch, we have roasted chicken and broccoli with black bean sauce and fried rice, and pork with noodles. Which one would you like?

Low-cost airlines

Low-cost airlines do not complimentary meals and beverages, and passengers are required to either pre-order their meal or purchase them on-board the flight. The cabin crew will first serve customers who have pre-ordered their meals according to the name list given by the ground agents or by cross-checking passengers' boarding pass against the flight plan. Cabin crew will make an announcement through the public announcement system to inform customers to have their boarding pass ready so that they can cross-check their boarding pass whilst serving the meals. Meals are also available for sale on-board low-cost flights.

Cabin crew: Ladies and gentlemen, the cabin crew will be offering in-flight meals in a short while. For those who are interested in ordering meals and beverages, please refer to the meal menu in the seat pocket in front of you. For passengers who have pre-ordered their meal, please have your boarding pass ready for the cabin crew's verification. Thank you.

Cabin crew will usually push the catering cart through the aisle and passengers who are interested in purchasing any food items can simply notify them.

Customer:	Excuse me, how much does a plate of chicken rice cost?
Cabin crew:	Five dollars, sir.
Customer:	Can I have one, please? I'd also like a coke.
Cabin crew:	Certainly, sir. Here are your chicken rice and coke. The total cost is seven dollars.
Customer:	Here you go.
Cabin crew:	Here is your change, sir. Thank you very much and enjoy your meal.

A special meal

A customer's travel agent forgot to make arrangements for her in-flight vegetarian meal and she was only notified during check-in at the departure gate. She was really upset as it was a long-haul flight, which meant that she would not be able to consume any food for the next 13 hours. As the plane was due to take off any minute, there was neither time for the airline to order a replacement special meal nor for the customer to get food from the airport's restaurants.

During the flight, the customer was surprised when the cabin crew offered her some salad and fruit. The cabin crew explained that the ground agent informed the other service agents and they managed to have these delivered over from the business-class lounge before the aircraft door was closed. The customer was extremely grateful that the airline had gone the extra mile.

DUTY-FREE SALES

Sales of duty-free items are only available on an international flight and this in-flight service is offered by both full service airlines and low-cost airlines. Duty-free sales are available after a meal service is completed and cabin crew will usually make an announcement to inform customers about the commencement of this service.

Cabin crew:	Ladies and gentlemen, duty-free sales are now available. There is a copy of the duty-free catalog in the seat pocket in front of you. Our cabin crew will be passing by your seats with the duty-free carts. Please feel free to let us know if you'd like to purchase any items. We accept most currencies and credit cards. Thank you.

Cabin crew must have some basic knowledge of every product featured on the catalog and be aware of the custom regulations of the destination country, especially in terms of the number of bottles of liquor and spirits allowed. The cabin crew should also alert passengers if they make purchases that are beyond the permitted quantity to avoid them getting into trouble with custom officers and airport security personnel.

Customer:	Excuse me. I would like to get this perfume.
Cabin crew:	Certainly, madam. Do you have a connecting flight at Hong Kong today?
Customer:	No, I don't.
Cabin crew:	Ok, that's great. This perfume is available in two sizes—250 ml and 350 ml. Would you like to get the bigger or smaller bottle?
Customer:	Hmm … I would like to buy the 350 ml bottle.
Cabin crew:	Sure. It would be 32 Euros. Would you like to pay by cash or credit card?
Customer:	Please charge it to my credit card.
Cabin crew:	Certainly, can I please have your signature?

Customer:	Excuse me. I would like to get this perfume.
Cabin crew:	Certainly, do you have a connecting flight at Hong Kong today?
Customer:	Yes, I do. I have a connecting flight to San Francisco.
Cabin crew:	I am sorry, Madam. This perfume is only available in two sizes—250 ml and 350 ml. I'd advise against purchasing the perfume on this flight as there will be another security check at Hong Kong Airport and all liquids that exceed 100 ml will be confiscated.
Customer:	Oh …
Cabin crew:	I suggest you that you purchase this perfume on-board the connecting flight to San Francisco instead.
Customer:	Sure. Thank you very much for your advice.

Cabin crew in-flight rest

To maintain a fresh appearance, cabin crew are allowed to take a short rest during long-haul flights. Most aircraft are equipped with a crew bunk where the cabin crew may take a break.

After resting, cabin crew must touch up on their makeup, adjust their hair and ensure that their uniform are neat and tidy before they return to the passenger cabin to continue their duties.

Figure 9-3: Cabin crew need to check their appearance before returning to duty.

Approaching the destination

Before an aircraft descends for landing, the cabin crew will secure the plane for arrival by making an announcement asking all passengers to return to their seats, fasten their seatbelts, put their seats and tray tables to the upright positions, store their baggage properly and open the window shades in preparation for landing.

Cabin crew: Ladies and gentlemen, our flight will be descending to Chengdu, People Republic of China in a moment. Please ensure that your seat belts are fastened and secure all baggage underneath your seats and in the overhead storage compartments.

Please ensure your seats and table trays are in the upright position for landing and open all window shades. Please also turn off all personal electronic devices, including laptops and mobile phones. Thank you.

Whilst the announcement is being made, other cabin crew make sure that passengers comply with the safety regulations.

Cabin crew: Excuse me, sir. Please fasten your seat belt. Thank you.
Excuse me, madam. Please place your handbag underneath the seat in front of you. Thank you.
Excuse me, sir. Please turn off your mobile phone. Thank you.

Landing at destination
After an aircraft has landed, the cabin crew will make an announcement providing some information about the destination's local time and weather conditions, and thank customers for choosing to fly with the airline. Cabin crew will also provide other information such as directions for connection flights, location for retrieving checked baggage as well as details pertaining to customs and immigration.

Cabin crew: Ladies and gentlemen, welcome to Chengdu Shuangliu
International Airport. The local time is 8:32 am and the
temperature is 25 Celsius or 77 Fahrenheit. For your safety
and comfort, please remain seated with your seat belt fastened
until the "fasten seat belt" sign is turned off.
Please be cautious when opening the overhead bins as your
belongings may have shifted during the flight. Please also
ensure that you have all your personal belongings with
you before leaving the aircraft.
You may retrieve your checked baggage at baggage belt
number 12. Please do not hesitate to contact our ground staff
if you require any assistance.
On behalf of C&M Airline and the entire crew, we'd like
to thank you for joining us on this trip. We look forward to
seeing you in the near future. Have a nice day.

Saying farewell

After an aircraft has come to a complete stop and is parked at the hanger,
passengers can then proceed to disembark. During this time, cabin crew
will be stationed by the exit to bid farewell to the customers. This helps to
enhance the customer relationship as a farewell helps to create a lasting
impression of an airline's services.[3] Cabin crew should make eye contact
with customers to demonstrate sincerity so that customers will feel that
they are valued and appreciated.

Figure 9-4: Cabin crew bidding farewell to customers.

Cabin crew: Goodbye, sir/madam.
Thank you and goodbye.
Thank you for flying with us.

"What would you like to drink, Ted?"

—by Ted Janusz[4]

Article reprinted with permission from Business 2 Community

"Huh?"

This evening on American flight 4105 from Columbus to Chicago, a flight attendant named Rebecca came down the aisle and addressed each passenger by name. I have been on over 1,000 flights and I have never seen or heard that before. So when Rebecca came to me and also addressed me by name, I was stunned.

So I asked her, "How do you do that?"

"It's easy," Rebecca replied. "I just read the manifest. I can't believe every flight attendant doesn't do it!"

In response, I told her that I deliver customer service training and asked if she could send me a "selfie" that I could use in my presentations, so she did.

Along with the photograph, she enclosed this note:

As an update to my story, I wanted to let you know that I continue to receive lots of positive letters from our passengers that rave about my use of their name when addressing them and my attitude! It is what keeps me going. Thank you for being an uplifting part of my life. You really made my day when I had you on my flight! I LOVE MY JOB!!!!

Best regards,
Rebecca

Even if you work in an industry not generally known for providing outstanding customer service, what ordinary thing could you do to become, like Rebecca—extraordinary? (In the process, you may find like Rebecca did, that you love your job!)

SUMMARY

The cabin crew plays an important in creating customer satisfaction. Cabin crew interact with customers during the entire duration of a flight, and are responsible for offering services and ensuring the safety of passengers. The functions of cabin crew include greeting customers as they board the aircraft, preparing the cabin for departure, offering in-flight service, preparing the cabin for landing and bidding farewell to customers. Whilst on-board the aircraft, the cabin crew must also resolve customers' problems and ensure that they have a pleasant and memorable flight.

APPLYING THE KNOWLEDGE

True or false?
Are the following statements true or false? Put a tick in the right column.

Statement	True	False
1. The primary duty of the cabin crew is to offer food to passengers.		
2. Customers judge cabin crew's professionalism based on their appearance.		
3. Pre-flight briefing allows cabin crew to understand more about customers prior to a flight.		
4. Cabin crew who are stationed by the entry during boarding are also known as "door persons".		
5. Safety demonstrations are not important and can be skipped on a connecting flight.		
6. First-class customers are more important than economy-class customers.		
7. Cabin crew use catering carts when offering meals to economy–class passengers.		
8. Duty-free sales are an integral part of an international flight's service.		
9. It is not necessary to thank customers during disembarkation as the in-flight service has ended.		
10. Customers with dietary restrictions are usually served last during an in-flight meal service.		

Multiple choice questions

1. A customer has asked for a cabin crew's assistance to help left a carry-on baggage for storage in the overhead compartment. How should the cabin crew respond?
   a. "That's your baggage. You need to do it by yourself."
   b. "I'm busy. You better ask another passenger to help you."
   c. "You should not carry this on-board the aircraft if you cannot lift it by yourself."
   d. "Sure. Let's lift it together."

2. How should a cabin crew respond when a customer requests for an aisle seat?
   a. "Please give me a moment. I will check if there are any available seats."
   b. "Sorry, this flight is full."
   c. "Please ask the passenger next to you if he or she would like to swop with you."
   d. "No, you can't. The flight is full."

3. How should a cabin crew respond when a customer requests for an additional glass of water during a busy meal service?
   a. "You can get it yourself from the galley."
   b. "Please give me a moment and I will bring it to you soonest."
   c. "Please wait. Can't you see that I am busy?"
   d. "I am busy. Can you please ask another cabin crew instead?"

4. How should a cabin crew respond when a customer complains about the lack of in-flight meal options?
   a. "My apologies. I am sorry about the limited choices available."
   b. "My apologies. I did not prepare the food."
   c. "I am sorry, but you either take it or leave it"
   d. "I am sorry, but that's all we have for this flight."

5. How should a cabin crew respond when a customer complains about the quality of the in-flight meal?
   a. "Really? I just had the same food and I think it's fine."
   b. "My apologies. Would you like to have a sandwich instead?"
   c. "That's normal. You're on an airplane, not in a restaurant."
   d. "You get what you pay for."

Short-answer questions

Imagine you are a member of a cabin crew. Rewrite the following questions
or sentences in full sentences so that they demonstrate professionalism
when interacting with passengers.

1. "We are taking off soon. Fasten your seat belt now."
2. "We only have fish left. You have no other choice."
3. "I don't have the perfume you want."
4. "Whose bag is this?"
5. "You cannot come inside the gallery."
6. "Hey, stop yelling at me."
7. "What's your problem?"
8. "Stop smoking in the toilet."
9. "Switch off your mobile phone now."
10. "Give me your trash."

ENDNOTES

1. Singapore Airlines. (2015). Singapore Girl. Singapore Airlines: http://www.singaporeair.com/en_UK/flying-with-us/singaporegirl/

2. *China Daily*. (2014, Oct 22). Survey: How nationality reflects flying habits. Asia one travel: http://travel.asiaone.com/article/news/survey-how-nationality-reflects-flying-habits

3. Evey, K. (2009, Oct 8). The Farewell is just as important as the Hello. Transforming the customer experience: http://www.kristinaevey.com/the-farewell-is-just-as-important-as-the-hello/

4. Janusz, T. (2013, Dec 3). Two Successful Customer Service Case Studies from (Surprise!) the Airlines. Business 2 Community: http://www.business2community.com/customer-experience/two-successful-customer-service-case-studies-surprise-airlines-0702586#ZgzUMBckXVAesdWR.99

CHAPTER TEN
Handling Customer Complaints

Chapter Outline

Learning Objectives

After reading this chapter, the reader should be able to:

- Understand why customers complain
- Recognize strategies for handling customer complaints
- Identify and recognize techniques to handle angry customers

CUSTOMER COMPLAINTS

While conflicts cannot be avoided in the service industry, the outcomes can be managed. In fact, customer complaints can be turned into opportunities for airlines to take in constructive feedback so to better improve their overall products and services. As such, every customer complaint must be treated with respect.

Customer complaints help an airline to:

- Improve its internal processes and procedures

Complaint	Possible cause of complaint
Waiting too long for the next available check-in counter	Inefficient queuing system or insufficient staff deployed
Not enough space to store hand-carry baggage	Airline staff are not complying with carry-on limitation policy

- Improve its products

Complaint	Possible cause of complaint
Seats are not comfortable	Other competitors offer better and more comfortable in-flight seats
In-flight entertainment system not operating properly	Maintenance department is not doing its job

- Understand customers' changing needs

Complaint	Possible cause of complaint
Lack of in-flight entertainment	Other competitors offer Wi-Fi services
Having to make a stopover	Airline does not offer non-stop flights

- Getting to know more about customers

Complaint	Possible cause of complaint
Unappetizing food	Taste of the food does not meet customers' expectations
Poor services provided by cabin crew	Airline does not have cabin crew members who can speak other languages

The US Department of Transportation has identified a list of common complaints made by airline customers and they are as follows:[1]

- **Flight problems**
  The majority of customers' complaints are pertaining to an airline's operations such as flight delays, cancellations, or failure to communicate information to passengers in advance.
- **Baggage**
  Many customers complain about mishandling of baggage. Majority of these complaints are filed at the baggage hall and are usually pertaining to late arrival of baggage or damaged baggage. Other baggage related issues include lack of storage for hand-carry items and charges for excess baggage.
- **Reservation, ticketing and boarding**
  Customer complaints pertaining to mistakes made by airline personnel usually include issues with ticket reservations, errors with issued tickets, check-in errors and other mistakes related to boarding of passengers.
- **Customer service**
  Customer complaints are usually related to employees' poor attitude, such as being rude or unhelpful. The bulk of these complaints occur in instances of flight delays whereby service agents are not helpful in terms of offering assistance.
- **Refunds**
  These pertain to inability of getting refunds for unused air tickets. This affects customers who have either changed their travel plans or missed their flights.
- **Poor amenities for the disabled**
  The majority of complaints involve lack of assistance extended to disabled customers. Some airlines do not provide adequate facilities and amenities for these passengers. There have also been isolated incidences where passengers have to pay a fee for using an airport's wheelchairs.

- **Over sales**
  Complaints made by affected customers who are not able to get a seat on a flight that they have confirmed reservation for due to overbooking. There are also occasions whereby customers are put on another flight, but a complaint is still made as their original travel plan may have been disrupted as a result.

- **Air fare**
  Apart from requesting for cheaper flight tickets, customers may also file complaints about incomplete information provided about airfare, and unreasonable travel conditions pegged to certain air fares.

- **Others**
  These include issues such as lax security, injuries caused due to air turbulence and problems with redeeming free tickets through airlines' frequent-flier programs.

- **Discrimination**
  These are usually related to disservices of customer of different gender, race and religious beliefs.

- **Breaking promises**
  Customers expect flights to take off on time and their assigned seats to be available. As such, they can get frustrated when these basic needs are not met.

- **Bad customer service**
  This usually pertains to dissatisfaction with long waiting time at the check-in counter, ease of locating and contacting service agents either in person or over the phone, and service agents' inability to offer solutions or unable to accede to requests.

- **Bad attitude**
  This includes interrupting customers when they are speaking, not listening or not being attentive to them or showing any signs of impatience and anger.

- **Hidden information**
  This happens when service agents fail to provide adequate information for customers to make informed decisions. Examples include offering similar type of air tickets at a lower price and being inconsistent when handling queries and requests.

- **Product malfunctions**

  This refers to malfunctioning of tangible products such as seats, tray tables, and in-flight entertainment system.

HANDLING CUSTOMER COMPLAINTS

Service agents have to interact with many customers in a single day. Many of the complaints are beyond these service agents' control and customers may sometimes be at fault. In spite of this, service agents need to identify customers' concerns and find ways to resolve their problems. The key to effective problem resolution is active listening, expressing concern, acknowledging the mistake, making apologies, analyzing the problem, demonstrating helpfulness, offering solutions and following up.

Active listening

It is important to listen to customers and to identify the cause of their unhappiness. While a customer is making a complaint, service agents should not interrupt them. Instead, they can either nod or make a verbal acknowledgement to let customers know that they are paying absolute attention to them in order to make them feel comfortable. Service agents should prioritize customers' feelings and do their best to put themselves in the customers' shoes so as to better understand the reasons for their frustration.

Service agents can ask themselves the following three simple questions:

- Why do passengers fly?
- What is the purpose of an airline?
- What are my responsibilities?

Answering these questions allows service agent to remain calm and to focus on their duties so that they can take the best course of actions to solve the problems. Service agents must not interrupt the customers and instead, allow them to finish what they want to say as these customers are usually firm about what needs to be conveyed to the service agents or even predict their responses. As such, even if the conversation does not turn out the way they have predicted, many of these customers will want to finish their thoughts without being interrupted, and cutting them will most likely result in a confrontational situation.

Express concerns

After customers have finished stating their concerns, service agents should seek to follow up with some questions to clarify any points that they are unsure of so as to avoid instances of miscommunication or misinterpretation. They can also choose to repeat or rephrase customers' complaints.

Acknowledge mistakes

Regardless of which party is at fault, service agents must acknowledge the mistake and inconvenience caused to customers as the first step to dealing with such tense situations. This can be done by responding with statements like the ones below:

- It appears that there is some miscommunication.
- I'm afraid our reservation department did not contact you.
- It seems that we are not performing to your expectations.

Apologize

Apologizing to customers is a demonstration of care and concern. Service agents should apologize regardless of which party is at fault.

Service agent: Please accept my apologies for this matter. Let me see what I can do to resolve this problem.

Analyze the problem

Once trust has developed between customers and service agents, and they are aware that service agents are doing their best to solve their problems, service agents can then focus on analyzing the situation and identify the root of the problem.

Demonstrate helpfulness

Service agents may sometimes require additional time to work out a viable solution as they need to consult other colleagues or check the system before proposing any alternative options. When dealing with customers who make complaints through phone, service agents should inform them the reason for putting them on hold and get their approval before doing so. Service agents should never reply customers' queries immediately, even if they already have an answer in mind as the customers may feel that the service agents are unhelpful and do not check with other sources before giving a response. By putting in extra time to work out a solution, this gives customers the sense that service agents are proactive and helpful in finding solutions.

Service agent: Mrs. Juliet, I understand how you feel.

Mrs. Juliet, I am sorry. This must be a disappointing experience for you.

Educate customers

On some occasions, complaints provide service agents with the opportunity to resolve any misunderstanding, and they can use such occasions to offer accurate and correct information to customers, and to clear up any potential confusion. This allows the airline to develop a better relationship with customers.

Work with customers

Involving customers in finding a solution is vital in developing a positive relationship between an airline and its customers as this indicates that service agents are sincere in helping them. As there isn't always a clear-cut solution to all problems, some service agents may need to consider other non-conventional options when handling some situations. As such, service agents must be well acquainted with an airline's policies and recognize the areas that allow room for flexibility. This allows service agents to come up with sound solutions for customers.

A quick fix to handling complaints regarding uncomfortable seats is a cabin upgrade. While this will definitely increase customers' level of satisfaction, an airline will end up losing its revenue as a premium seat will then no longer be available for sale. As such, service agents should seek to resolve the issue by first offering another seat in the same cabin class.

Providing solutions

There are times that the solution provided by an airline might not be what customers expect. As such, service agents should provide full explanations as to why a proposed solution is made in the customer's interest. If the situation permits, customers should be informed about the various options available so that they can choose the one that best suits their needs.

Service agent: I apologized to Mr. Williamson as his business-class seat was broken. In return, Mr. Williamson requested for a free upgrade. Unfortunately, the first-class cabin was completely full. After a long discussion, Mr. Williamson accepted my proposed offer of a downgrade to economy class with a seat in an empty row on top of an additional 5,000 miles credit in his frequent flyer account.

Improve the situation

On occasions whereby customers' demands cannot be met or fall outside the company's policy, service agents should provide a valid and sound explanation, offer alternatives and apologize.

Service agent: I am sorry that the flight has been delayed for 3 hours.

Customer: Well ... how are you going to compensate the three hours of my life that I have spent waiting to board the plane?

Service agent: My apologies, sir. May I offer you a free upgrade to business class instead?

Service agent: I apologize that the flight has been cancelled.

Customer: I have a very important meeting to attend. Fly me on a private jet instead.

Service agent: My apologies, sir. I am unable to do that. Can I offer you a seat on another flight to Singapore instead?

Make promises

If an issue cannot be resolved immediately, service agents can choose to inform customers that they will follow up shortly. However, they should make all efforts to keep to their promises to avoid further antagonizing disgruntled customers.

Request for service agent's name

Customers have a tendency to ask service agents for their names either to pressure the them to give in to their demands or for the purpose of lodging future complaints. Airline frontline staff should comply with such requests politely at all times.

Customer: What is your name? I am going to lodge a complaint about you.

Service agent: My name is Sophia Wang.

Request to talk to superiors

Some demanding customers may not trust service agents' ability in solving their problems and prefer to speak directly to someone with more authority such as a supervisor or a manager. In such incidents, service agents should explain the situation to their superior so that they can best deal with the issue and to avoid having customers repeat themselves again.

At the same time, superiors should gather as much information as possible before approaching customers. This will help to speed up the discussion and to minimize customers' waiting time.

There have been many occasions in which customers may relent when service agents' managers provide the same responses. This is especially so when their intention is to check with someone with more authority to ensure that the service staff have done their due diligence.

Excuse from tense situations

When dealing with unreasonable or aggressive customers, service agents are recommended to excuse themselves from the scene thereafter and take some time to calm down and sort out their emotions before serving other customers.

In instances whereby service agents are unable to control their emotions, they should request for their colleagues to take over and handle the particular difficult situation rather than risk being curt or rude to customers. Service agents may even be asked to justify their bad attitude and behavior if customers lodge a complaint against them.

Wrap-up

Apologizing to customers for the inconvenience caused and thanking them for their businesses serve to portray a positive image of an airline. Ending the conversation with a friendly 'thank you' is a way of showing appreciation to customers who have raised their concerns.

Record the incidents

All complaint incidents must be recorded into the passenger name record (PNR), regardless of whether they have been resolved. This can be in the form of a written report submitted to the supervisor, and the information will be available to another service agent for future follow-up. Service agents and all related personnel are recommended to submit a detailed incident report as soon as a complaint has been lodged.

OTHER PLATFORMS FOR LODGING COMPLAINTS

Apart from face-to-face communication and telephone conversations, customers voice their concerns via other avenues such as email or social media. Service agents must respond to customers in a timely manner and ensure their needs are addressed.

Read the message
It is important for service agents to identify and address the cause of customers' complaints. As such, they should read the entire message before replying.

Begin an email/reply
Begin the reply with a 'thank you' to show appreciation for the feedback. This helps to restore customers' confidence in the airline and regain their goodwill.

Apologize
Service agents must apologize to customers if an airline is at fault. This demonstrates the airline is responsible and holds itself accountable for the errors. It is especially important when customers make the complaints through social media. Issuing a public apology also prevents customer escalation and dissatisfaction.

Provide an explanation
Explaining the cause of the problem helps to re-establish trust. This also shows that service agents offer personalized services.

Offer gestures of goodwill
In instances whereby an airline is at fault, service agents should offer a gesture of goodwill. These can be in the form of discounted coupons, cash vouchers or free air miles. Offering gestures of goodwill helps to re-build customers' level of trust and confidence.

Service agent: My apologies about the delay, Ms. Sharon. Once again, thank you for your kind understanding and for choosing our airline.

Identify the problem
- Active listening
- Express concern
- Accept mistake
- Apologize

Understand the problem
- Analyze the problem
- Demonstrate helpfulness

Work out the solution
- Work with customer
- Offer solution
- Wrap-up

Figure 10-1: Customer problem resolution.

TURNING COMPLAINTS INTO OPPORTUNITIES

Successfully handling of complaints can turn the customers' dissatisfaction into opportunities. Some customers complain about the airline operations and its product.

On some occasions, service agents may choose to upsell these customers. This is a sales technique that many airlines use to induce customers to purchase more expensive items, upgrades, or other add-ons in an attempt to make a more profitable sale. Within the airline industry, this usually pertains to an existing product or an upgrade to a better travel class. For instance, if customers complain about their assigned seats, service agent may suggest an upsell by proposing an upgrade to business class or a better seat in premium economy class. As such, even though there are no better seating options in the economy class, upselling provides these customers with another choice. This also gives the airline an opportunity to increase their sales.

A passenger in wheelchair was travelling from the Amami Islands to Osaka. A service agent told him that he would not be able to fly if he could not walk up the stairs. According to the airline's strict safety rules, his friends were not allowed to help him even though they were traveling together. In order to board the plane, he had to climb up the flight of stairs using his arms. News of this incident spread quickly and the airline management team eventually issued an apology to the passenger and promised to take corrective actions to upgrade its facilities at all airports to better assist disabled customers.

IDENTIFYING ANGRY CUSTOMERS

Anger is an intense emotional response that involves a strong response to a perceived provocation or threat. It occurs when a person feels their personal boundaries are being violated. It can also be a protective mechanism to cover up signs of fear, hurt or sadness.[2] In addition, anger can be triggered by external factors such as frustration, feeling of unfairness, and verbal and physical abuse.

Unlike upset customers who might be mildly displeased about something, angry customers often display frustration, aggressiveness and impatience when interacting with service agents. This is one of the most challenging duties of service agents and they have to demonstrate their professionalism at all times. Service agents should always remain calm, defuse customers' anger, identify the cause of their annoyance and offer assistance as much as possible. The following are some giveaway signs and behaviors of angry customers:

- **Raising their voice**
  Angry customers can be loud and may even yell at times. They may also instruct service agents and order them around.
- **Provoking service agents**
  Some customers may resort to offensive speech or actions in order to provoke and spite service agents into giving in.
- **Interrupt others**
  They usually cut service agents off mid-sentence.
- **Taking control over the conversation**
  These customers have the tendency to keep talking and are focused on making a point. They neither listen to others nor allow them to speak.

- **Threaten to speak to superiors**

  They may threaten to speak to someone with more authority if they do not get what they want or if a situation is not handled to their satisfaction.

Handling angry customers
Isolation

It is always a good idea to invite these customers to an area such as the aircraft's gallery or a separate room that is away from the check-in counter where the issue can be sorted out privately. This allows the discussion to take place without disturbing other customers.

Figure 10-2: Do not show defensive gestures when handling angry customers.

Remain calm

Remaining calm is key to handling angry customers. Service agents must remain calm at all times and refrain from yelling back or showing anger as doing so will only worsen the situation and customers may even complain about service agents' attitude.

The customer is always right

Service agent should never seek to win an argument with customers and this will reflect badly on an airline.

Dealing with confrontations

Service agents must pay extra attention to this group of customers. Some customers may use unpleasant words when expressing their frustration and service agents should not take this personally. Instead, they need to focus on identifying customers' source of anger whilst maintaining a friendly attitude. However, if a customer becomes abusive, service agents should not hesitate to remind them politely that their behavior is unwarranted, and that customers using abusive language or gesture can be prosecuted.

In such instances, service agents should refrain from further interaction with such customers and request for law enforcement officers to come in and sort out the situation. It is not always easy to communicate with agitated customers. Myra Golden Media, a customer service and public relations agency that specializes in strategic customer relations consulting has suggested two several tested and proven strategies that service agents can adopt in such situations.[3]

- **"Kill Them with Diplomacy"**
  Service agents should seek to show empathy by putting themselves in the same situation as customers and address them in a direct and non-defensive manner. This helps to prevent any further confrontation.

- **Go into "computer mode"**
  Service agents are advised to go into "computer mode" when dealing with angry customers. This nautical mode is similar to an automated response system that is devoid of any emotions. Doing so helps to diffuse and disarm angry customers without involving their personal feelings. This also allows service agents to be emotionally in control of the situation.

Reminder to customers

Many customers get irritated when they do not get what they want. They will often blame service agents for not being helpful and even end up verbally attacking them. At these times, service agents need to remind such customers about their behavior. Service agent can use some phases to let the customer know that while they can complain about a problem, it should not be extended to personal insults. Doing so forces customers to calm down and focus on the actual problem.

Service agent: I am sorry that we've upset you. I understand how you feel and I would be equally upset if I were in your position.

Jenny is a service agent on duty at the check-in counter. She realized that one of the passenger's check-in baggage has exceeded the weight limit.

Service agent: Excuse me, Mr. Yamamoto. The baggage allowance is 20 kilograms but your baggage is 27 kilograms.

Customer: So?

Service agent: Mr. Yamamoto, I am afraid that I will need to ask you to either repack your baggage and remove unnecessary items or pay for the excess baggage weight.

Customer: This is ridiculous. I want to speak to your supervisor.

Service agent: Sure. One moment, please.

Jenny approached Jonathan, her supervisor and explained the situation to him. Jonathan then spoke to Mr. Yamamoto.

Supervisor: Good morning, Mr. Yamamoto, my name is Jonathan, the supervisor on duty today. What I can do for you?

Customer: I am not happy with your staff. She has asked me to either repack my belonging or pay for the excess baggage. I have been travelling in this manner for so many years and have never had a problem.

Supervisor: Mr. Yamamoto, I understand the situation and thank you for letting me know about your past traveling experience. According to our airline's policy, you are entitled to 20 kg of check-in baggage and it has now exceeded by 7 kg. I've noticed you do not have any carry-on baggage with you. Would you reconsider repacking your luggage if we provide you with a free carry-on bag? That case, you won't need to pay for the excess baggage.

Customer: All right. I will repack, but I am still not happy with your airline's policy. You should feedback this to your manager.

Supervisor: I understand how you feel and thank you for your feedback. Please wait a moment. I'll get you a bag for your carry-on items.

> *Jonathan returned with a shopping bag and Mr. Yamamoto repacked his baggage.*
>
> **Supervisor:**   Mr. Yamamoto, thank you for your understanding. We wish
>   you a pleasant flight.

Show appreciation

Thank customers for spending their valuable time to give a feedback as most customers do not expect service agents to express their appreciation after they have lodged a complaint. This is an effective strategy for getting agitated customers to calm down so that service agents can take over the situation and focus on problem resolution.

Dos and Don'ts

Do ...	Don't ...
Listen to the customer	Get defensive
Apologize	Argue with customers
Acknowledge the mistake	Show anger
Remain calm	Show sarcasm
Show empathy	Request customers to repeat themselves
Offer solution and options	Leave customers waiting
Turn complaints to opportunities	Emphasize the need to abide by the airline's policy

Terminate the conversation

If the conversation does not result in any conflict resolution and customers continue to abuse service agents verbally and physically, service agents can choose to end the discussion, suspend the service or issue a warning. If the customers are on the phone, service agents can politely inform them that they can no longer help them and will proceed to terminate the call. When dealing with face-to-face interactions, service agents may politely request for customers to leave the airport premises. If these customers' unruly behavior continues, service agents can then request for help from other staff or call in law enforcement offices as a last resort.

Customer:	What the #$@&%*!
Service agent:	My apologies, Mr. Chen, I am afraid that we cannot continue this conversation with your current behavior. I am sorry to inform you that I will need to hang up the phone now and I will get my supervisor to contact you shortly. Thank you for calling.

Official complaints

If frontline staff members have tried all possible solutions to handle customers' concerns but are unable to come to any resolution or if a customer has made an impossible request, the staff may suggest for them to lodge an official complaint with the airline either via a written letter or email. Their concerns will then be addressed by the respective customer relations department. Service agents should also avoid using the word "complaint" to avoid further agitating these customers.

Customer:	I am unhappy with how you've handled the situation. I demand my compensation right now.
Service agent:	I understand your concerns. Unfortunately, I am unable to offer you compensation at this moment. May I suggest for you to contact the customer relations department for this matter? You can reach them at …

Lawsuits

Some angry customers may threaten to sue an airline or its staff as a last resort. When dealing with such scenarios, service agents should remain claim and refer these customers to the respective customer relations department rather than attempting to sort out the matter on their own.

Customer: I am going to sue your company.

Service agent: I understand your concerns. May I suggest for you to contact the customer relations department for this matter. You can reach them at ....

ANGER MANAGEMENT FOR SERVICE AGENTS

It is important for service agents to be able to control their emotions, especially any feelings of unhappiness or anger. They should not lose their temper even if the customers are clearly at fault. Service agents should seek to control over their anger and handle an unpleasant situation by tapping on their emotional intelligence (EQ). A person with a high EQ is able to read the facial and emotional cues of another person and react accordingly.

There are no doubt occasions whereby service agents may be frustrated with customers or their unreasonable requests. Rather than showing any signs of annoyance, service agents should take a step back and ask themselves the following questions:

1. Why am I acting in this particular manner?
2. Why do I feel annoyed/upset/frustrated?
3. Should I react this way?
4. Will I resolve the problem in this manner?

Think before speaking
It is inevitable for individuals to say something that they may regret during confrontations. To avoid such incidents, service agents should take a few moments to think before responding.

Do not take things personally
Some customers may try to provoke service agents to react aggressively and lodge further complains about their poor attitude. As such, service agent must not take these issues personally.

Relax

Taking a deep breath often works wonders in calming a person down. Service agents can remind themselves to stay calm and maintain their professionalism by using some catchphrases or words such as "Stay relaxed", "Keep calm" or "Stay chill" whilst taking a deep breath.

Focus on the goal

Service agents should always focus on their goal of helping customers. Customers are usually angry because they have encountered tricky situations and service agents should endeavor to help them sort these out in the shortest time possible.

Share experiences

Sharing a particular frustrating incident with someone else in the same industry often helps one to calm down and even better understand a customer's point of view. As such, it is recommended for service agents to excuse themselves after they have dealt with an unpleasant incident and share it with a friend, colleague or counselor.

Write it down

Anger can be also released through writing. Many people write complaint letters or emails as a form of anger expression and there have been numerous occasions whereby these letters were not sent out as the feelings of resentment or frustration have already been vented out. Writing an unpleasant situation down may even allow one to look at the same issue from a new perspective.

SUMMARY

It is common for airline companies to receive complaints from unhappy customers. Service agents should treat each complaint seriously and try to resolve them to customers' satisfaction. On many occasions, complaints can be turned to opportunities and frustrated passengers converted to loyal customers. Effective handling of complaints requires excellent communication and problem-solving skills. This is especially so when dealing with angry customers as service agents must remain calm at all times. When confronted with difficult situations, service agents must learn to manage their emotions and respond in a manner that is in the best interest of an airline.

APPLYING THE KNOWLEDGE

Read the scenarios below. Then answer the respective follow-up questions in complete sentences.

1. The following conversation takes place during check-in:

Customer:	Can you block the seat next to mine and keep it empty?
Ground service agent:	Of course, sir. Today's flight is not full and we are able to do so.
Customer:	Thank you.
Ground service agent:	You're welcome.

    While on the plane, the customer notices a mother with a newborn baby sitting in the seat next to his. He then calls for the cabin crew.

Customer:	Excuse me, why is there someone seated next to me? I was told that the seat next to mine would be empty.
Cabin crew:	I am afraid there has been some miscommunication. Today's flight is completely full and there are no empty seats.
Customer:	But I was told otherwise and the lady at the check-in counter promised to keep this seat empty.
Cabin crew:	My apologies, sir. The flight is completely full and we are about to take off.

    a. Why is the customer dissatisfied?
    b. Do you think the ground service agent's response is appropriate? If yes, explain why. If not, how should the agent have responded?

2. A passenger pushes the flight attendant call button shortly after the plane has taken off.

Customer: Excuse me, there is something wrong with my seat. It cannot recline fully.

Cabin crew: Hi, sir. Could you please step away from your seat so that I can find out what's wrong with it?

Customer: Yes, of course. Thank you.

The cabin crew tested the seat and there was no problem with it.

Customer: No, it is still not right. This seat does not recline fully. Is it possible to change my seat?

Cabin crew: I am sorry, sir. The economy class is completely full.

Customer: Well … since your seat is not working, you should offer me a seat in business class instead.

Cabin crew: _____.

a. Why is the customer dissatisfied?

b. Imagine you are the cabin crew. How would you respond to the customer's request for an upgrade to the business-class cabin?

3. Imagine you are a manager of an airline's customer relations department. You have just received the following letter:

Attn:

Customer Service Manager

C&M Airline

455 Joan Ave

Barangay, Manila

March 23, 2017

Dear Sir/Madam

  I am writing today to complain about your company false statement. I recently purchased a round trip ticket from C&M Airline for Flight #9422/9421 Manila to Honolulu for $1230. 90. I called your airline's reservation center to reserve an aisle seat and was informed by your agent that I had to call A&B Airline instead as this is a codeshare flight.

I have chosen to fly with C&M Airline because of your reputation for providing excellent services. I was very disappointed after learning that your company has sold me a seat at a premium price, but with sub-standard service provided by A&B Airline's service crew.

I have specifically avoided A&B Airline due to my previous bad experience with the airline, even though the airfare for the same route is $120 cheaper.

I am very disappointed with your company's false advertising for a flight that doesn't exist and that you are charging your customers a premium price for a service that is available at a much cheaper rate.

As such, I am writing to demand a refund of $120 from your company since I am now stuck with this flight and have been informed by your agents that a full ticket refund is not available. I look forward to hearing from you.

Yours sincerely,
Samuel Beckham

a. Why is the customer dissatisfied?
b. Write a reply of no more than 300 words.

ENDNOTES

1. Boston.com. Top 10 complaints of airline passengers. Boston.com: http://www.boston.com/business/gallery/airline_passenger_complaints/

2. The emotional life. (2011). What is anger? The emotional life: http://www.pbs.org/thisemotionallife/topic/anger/what-anger

3. Golden, M. (2010, Jan 27). How to Get Any Angry Customer to Back Down. Myra Golden Media: https://myragolden.wordpress.com/2010/01/27/how-to-get-any-angry-customer-to-back-down/

CHAPTER ELEVEN

Evaluating Customer Service

Chapter Outline

Learning Objectives

After reading this chapter, the reader should be able to:

- Understand service quality management
- Understand various ways an airline can evaluate customer service standards
- Recognize mystery shoppers

SERVICE QUALITY MANAGEMENT

It is important for an airline to manage the quality of its products and service, especially in a market where customers' preferences are changing rapidly. Airlines need to understand customers and their expectations. To evaluate whether an airline's services are meeting customers' expectations, it needs to carry out various service quality management programs.
The process of managing the quality of services delivered to customers according to their expectations is called service quality management. It assesses how well a service has been given, and the purpose is to improve its quality of products, identify problems and correct them to increase customer satisfaction. Service quality management includes monitoring and maintenance of the varied services that are offered to customers by an airline, with the eventual goal of helping it to achieve its financial targets.

EVALUATING CUSTOMER SERVICE

An airline's management uses various methods to track the quality of customer service performance so as to understand customer satisfaction level and to identify potential problems. Airlines often develop standards and guidelines for frontline employees to ensure that a minimum standard of customer service. These guidelines are as follows:

Customer care center
- Customer waiting time before an agent answers a call
- Duration of the call time spent with each customer
- Professionalism of service agent in terms of knowledge and service attitude

Check-in counter
- Customer waiting time in the lobby
- Check-in processing time
- Professionalism of service agent in terms of knowledge and service attitude

Lounge

- Cleanliness
- Types of refreshments available
- Quantity of refreshments available

Boarding gate

- Required boarding time
- Push back time
- Professionalism of service agent in terms of knowledge and service attitude

In-flight:

- Cleanliness of cabin
- Defects in facilities and amenities
- Variety of food and beverages offered
- Professionalism of cabin crew in terms of knowledge and service attitude

Arrival and baggage:

- Frequency of baggage irregularities
- Frequency of baggage damage

Customer contact center

A study on waiting time has indicated that the average waiting time for a call center, regardless of a company's size, is 7 minutes and 19 seconds.[1]

Below is a list of holding time of some major airlines that fly into the North American continent according to FastCustomer, a service provider[2]

Airline *all data accurate as of September 2016	Average waiting time
Air Canada	8 minutes and 39 seconds
Air France	1 minutes and 53 seconds
American Airlines	5 minutes and 50 seconds
British Airways	4 minutes and 04 seconds
Delta Airlines	6 minutes and 47 seconds

(Continued)

Airline *all data accurate as of September 2016	Average waiting time
Korean Air	1 minutes and 58 seconds
Singapore Airlines	2 minutes and 36 seconds
Southwest Airlines	12 minutes and 52 seconds
United Airlines	5 minutes and 23 seconds
WestJet	7 minutes and 17 seconds

*All data accurate as of 22 December 2017.

The length of waiting time is mainly dependent on volume of incoming calls and number of service agents deployed. These statistics allow an airline's management to identify any potential problems with the process in cases whereby the waiting time is increased so that such issues can be resolved soonest.

Call abandonment rate

The abandonment rate measures the percentage of incoming callers who choose to hang up before their call is answered due to prolonged waiting time. A survey completed by the American multinational financial services corporation, American Express in 2012 has noted that the maximum period of time a customer is willing to wait over the phone for assistance is approximately 12 minutes.[3] As such, it is important for airlines to ensure that all phone calls can be attended to during this period to avoid customer disservice and turning away of potential customers.

Customer care center performance

Service agents located in the customer care center can be assessed by reviewing recorded conversations. The recording process takes place right before customers are connected to a service agent, and they will usually hear the following message: "Thank you for waiting, this call may be monitored or recorded for quality assurance purposes. If you decided not participate, please press 1. You are now connected to a service agent." Supervisors can then monitor servicing staff performance by listening to the playbacks and find out areas for improvement.

Managers or supervisors can also be mystery customers by calling the customer care center. This will give the management team in-depth data about the waiting time and service agents' performance. The professionalism of service agents and customer relationship skills such as attitude, knowledge and problem-solving skills can be also tested through direct conversations.

Check-in counter performance

Performance at the check-in counter is affected by both environment and the ability of an airline service agent. The environment of the check-in counter setup has a direct impact on the customer waiting time, while the level of efficiency and courtesy demonstrated by service agents influence customer satisfaction.

Waiting time
Check- in queue

Customers expect to be served as soon as they arrive at the airport for check in. The customer waiting time is measured from the time customers enter the check-in area until the moment they are attended to by a service agent. This waiting time varies according to airline counters' setup. Due to different customer expectations, many airlines now offer different check-in areas for customers according to the types of cabins. The queuing system that the airline deploys also has an impact on the waiting time as the use of individual and the common queuing system can affect the queue waiting time. However, the required space for these queuing systems' setups and the queue capacity for the respective check-in counters vary according to airlines.

The waiting time always seems shorter when a line keeps moving.[4] According to an air travelers experience survey conducted by ORC International for Civil Aviation Authority UK at Heathrow, Gatwick, Stansted and Manchester airports, a customer's maximum expectation time for checking in is 20 minutes, regardless of whether they are traveling on full service airlines or low-cost carriers.[5]

The waiting time is also an indication of whether enough check-in counters are available and how fast check-in agents attend to customers.

Check-in agents' performance

Check-in agents' performance can be measured by technology and through observation. In terms of technology, performances can be evaluated using the departure control system (DCS) which calculates service agents' efficiency by measuring the check-in process time. The system measures the start and end time of each customer. A report is then generated to indicate the average check-in time taken by each agent and the number of customers processed by a particular agent during a specific timeframe.

Boarding gate performance

Both check-in counters and boarding gates are monitored by airport managers and supervisors to ensure service agents maintain an expected level of service.

The amount of time required to complete the boarding process has a direct impact on the on- time departure of a flight. As such, airlines pay special attention to boarding gate performances. This is measured by calculating the total boarding time taken for passengers to board a flight. The DCS records the time the first customer boards the plane until the last customer's embarkation. The boarding time can range between 30 to 45 minutes, depending on the type of aircraft. The DCS then makes an evaluation taking into consideration other factors such as the number of customers who have checked in, the aircraft's parking location and the type of boarding gate used.

During boarding, the majority of airlines segregate customers into different groups. The evaluator then assesses a service agent's performance for boarding management. As such, service agents should follow an airline's boarding policy so as to speed up the boarding process. Failure to do so may result in congestion and chaos inside the aircraft cabin.

In-flight service performance

In-flight service performance can be monitored by a purser who serves as the manager or a supervisor. Some airlines hire internal auditors on-board flights. These auditors are tasked to inspect cabin crews' performance. Cabin crew members are assessed based on their service attitude, together with their ability to deliver safety knowledge to customers and how well they conduct safety demonstrations.

Baggage performance

Upon arrival at a destination, customers expect their baggage to be ready for collection in the baggage hall, and this contributes to the overall customer satisfaction experience. As such, some airlines have started a program that guarantees their customers are able to retrieve their baggage within 20 minutes upon a flight's arrival and compensation will be offered in instances when the waiting time exceeds that. This has in turn become the industry's standard.

Customer satisfaction with regard to baggage delivery also includes the ratio of delay, lost and damaged baggage. According to SITA's 2015 baggage report, a total of 24.1 million bags were mishandled in 2014 and the industry's average number of mishandled baggage is 7.3 bags per 1,000 customers.[6]

Service agents' performance in the baggage hall is monitored by both airport managers and supervisors. Indicators for monitoring service agents' performance include interactions with customers, proactiveness and efficiency in helping customers track missing baggage as well as following-up.

MEASURING CUSTOMER SATISFACTION

Airlines use multiple methods to evaluate customer satisfaction level and the services provided.

Mystery shopper programs

Some airlines use mystery shopper programs to collect data for measuring service quality. A mystery shopper program is a customer satisfaction measuring tool that gives companies in-depth findings about the quality of the service offered, service agents' attitude, service agents' compliance with the airlines' policy and their ability to resolve problems. Feedback received via such programs usually includes details that cannot be obtained through normal surveys.

Mystery shoppers are also known as consumer shoppers. They hide their identities and use an airline's services just like normal customers. These mystery shoppers observe service agents' behavior, ask questions, and may even create some difficult situations or even lodge unreasonable complaints to assess their ability to resolve these issues. The mystery shoppers then document the necessary information for review purposes and airlines can take the corresponding corrective actions. Many international airlines have opted to use a mystery shopper program. Air France KLM has even reportedly asked a few members of its Flying Blue loyalty program to audit the service standards on some of their flights.

Air France KLM "employs" frequent flyers as mystery shoppers[7]

—By Raymond Kollau

Article reprinted with permission from airlinetrends.com

Air France KLM 'Quality Observers'

Many airlines employ mystery flyers in return for valuable insight into the daily runnings of flights provide undercover flyers with a free flight and paid-for expenses.

Air France KLM has come up with an innovative twist for its mystery flyers program and is introducing a new so-called "Quality Observer" program. Instead of employing mystery shoppers, the Quality Observers are recruited from the airlines' community of Flying Blue members.

Within the program, Elite members from the airlines' Flying Blue loyalty program will be randomly invited to join the Quality Observer community and participate as mystery flyers during their travel, according to booking data and the pre-set Quality Observer coverage and frequency needs per station.

This joint Air France KLM program is designed to objectively observe and measure if product and services are delivered according to pre-set specifications at every customer point of contact during the actual journey (booking/call centers are planned to be added next year). According to Air France KLM, the aim of the Quality Observer program is to ensure a worldwide consistency in [terms of] quality of service delivered to its passengers.

Mobile app

A special Quality Observer app (both for iOS and Android devices) is made available for the Quality Observers. To use the application, Flying Blue members need to be registered as a Quality Observer with AFKL, which is by invitation only.

The app contains a questionnaire to allow Quality Observers to assess the compliance of the quality of service in airport and in-flight. The main touch points to be observed—both on a product and service level—are: Check-in, Lounge, Boarding, In-flight, Transfer and Arrival. Besides objective—YES/NO—and actionable questions, the Quality Observer can also include a small comment in case of a non-conformity situation and in selected situations where no staff or passengers are involved, add a photo to better illustrate their observation.

Quality Observers will be offered an incentive (Flying Blue Award Miles) when they have completed all questions and a special website has been designed to keep Quality Observers informed about and engaged in the program (so that experienced members will serve as Quality Observer regularly).

Regular assessments, digital feedback

According to AFKL, the main advantages of the Quality Observer initiative compared to the former Mystery Shopper program are that all destinations and classes are now being assessed on a regular (weekly) basis, results are delivered promptly, there is more flexibility for ad-hoc audits (for example when introducing a new product on board), and the airlines save on the ticket costs involved.

A small-scale start of the program with 600 participants starts in mid-October and a full roll-out is planned in January 2014.

Air France KLM stresses that Quality Observers are informed that their mystery flyer status does not confer any right with respect to their treatment by the airline during their journey and that they are subject to the same regulations that apply to all passengers.

Satisfaction surveys

Satisfaction surveys allow an airline to understand its current performance and how well it meets customers' expectations. It also allows the airline to better track changes in customers' demand. Airlines may choose to conduct an in-flight survey; selected customers are selected to complete a questionnaire. Many airlines prefer to survey frequent travelers during a flight as these customers have a higher tendency to give information about their opinion on the airlines' performance, as well as their competitors.

A customer satisfaction survey can include questions covering the entire travel process, from ticket reservation to the entire check-in experience at an airport. Other areas surveyed include in-flight experience, such as aspects related to cabin crew's service attitude, meal service and environment within an aircraft such as layout, whether the seats are comfortable and cleanliness.[8] Below is a detailed breakdown of items that are usually measured in a satisfaction survey:

Product	Overall quality of product/Design of in-flight product
Delivery process	Speed of check-in process
	Speed of boarding a flight
	Satisfaction with in-flight service
	Speed of baggage delivery upon arrival
Staff and service	Servicing staff's availability
	Serving staff's knowledge
	Courteousness of service agents
	Friendliness of service agents
	Complaint resolution performance
	Responsiveness to enquiries
Airline	Reputation of airline
Price	Value for money
	Price of air tickets as compared to other airlines offering similar services

Focus groups and in-depth interviews

Some airlines may invite customers to take part in focus group meetings. Focus group meetings allow airlines to obtain detailed information from different customer types and their satisfaction with regard to the airlines' services and products. Airlines may invite both frequent flyers and infrequent flyers to attend a meeting in which the moderator will ask them some questions. These customers will then share their thoughts through discussions.

In-depth one-on-one interview with individual customers is another way that allows airline to obtain more information about customers' demands and their level of satisfaction. Airlines can get detailed information such as the quality of the food served on- board a flight, and in-flight facilities and amenities, such as the entertainment system, reading material and toiletries.

Social media

Social media such as Twitter and Feedback are playing an increasingly important role in helping airlines to collect unsolicited information from customers though online forums and social media platforms. Many travel websites now encourage customers to review their travel experiences and airlines often dedicate personnel to monitor these websites so as to gather both positive and negative feedback. Monitoring social media platforms helps airline management teams to better understand an airline's day-to-day business and to gain insight into customers' expectations. Customers' personal details such as travel habits may also be obtained through social media platforms.[9]

CUSTOMER RELATIONSHIP MANAGEMENT

Data collected from the above-mentioned sources are analyzed and used by an airline to improve its operations, as well as to keep a check on its competitor's services and products. The table below shows some examples of comments given by customers and how an airline turns them into action points through the following:

- Identify different sources and channels that can help understand customers
- Recognize the changes in customers' values
- Understand the customer value in building loyalty
- Examine how various technology can increase customer satisfaction.

Comments from customers	Action taken by airline
"I waited a long time before someone at the service center picked up my phone call."	Identify the problem and increase manpower at the call center
"The waiting line at the check-in counter is too long."	Increase the number of check-in kiosk machines or come up with new online check-in applications
"The boarding gate is messy."	Separate customers into different groups during boarding

(Continued)

Comments from customers	Action taken by airline
"The airline run out of the meal of my choice."	Look into the percentage of each food choice selected by passengers and adjust the proportions accordingly
"The projector on the in-flight entertainment system is not clear."	Install a personal entertainment system for all passengers
"It takes a long time for me to retrieve my baggage."	Review the baggage delivery process and find ways to improve it

CUSTOMER SATISFACTION MANAGEMENT

Voice of Customer Management System in Operation

—Asiana Airlines[10]

Article reprinted with permission from Asiana Airlines

In January 2013, Asiana Airlines opened its New VOC System after improving its VOC processing capacity, building customer complaint prevention measures and renewing a strategic VOC management system for efficient, effective service quality management and adjusting any inappropriate services.

Also, we have set CSI: Customer Satisfaction Index and Customer Complaint Index as our major management indices for customer satisfaction management, reflecting the results as main PM criteria when evaluating CEO and executive performances to realize a service responsibility management in which all executives and employees are held responsible for service quality.

Any complaints or inconveniences issued and suggested by customers are dealt with in real time at "Customer Complaint One Stop Processing Service". The operation of "Customer Complaint Reward Standards", which reflects the needs of the customers has contributed greatly to enhancing customer loyalty.

Efforts to enhance customer satisfaction

Enhancement of service quality through operation of All-employee Service Quality Inspection System Asiana Airlines operates various "service quality inspection systems" to evaluate and manage efficient service quality. The results of service quality inspections conducted by service quality experts in numerous service locations and flight inspections conducted by all employees upon their business trips are reported to the CEO and related departments, and used as real time service quality enhancement data. In particular, the domestic/international airline quality monitoring conducted by all employees is used as a major means when establishing our differentiation strategy.

Enhancement of service quality through customer satisfaction survey

Asiana Airlines regularly conducts an "on/offline customer satisfaction level" survey to recognize overall service quality standards and customer needs. The customer satisfaction level survey of our members and customers who visit our homepage as well as domestic/international service quality evaluation organizations' service quality inspection and audit, etc., are carried out to analyze our service quality. The results are frequently utilized as service enhancement data, and we continuously strive to provide world-class services to our customers.

Company meetings are operated for service quality management

As the highest decision making organization, Asiana Airlines regularly holds/operates a "Customer Satisfaction Enhancement Council" composed of executives, related management, and heads of departments to make decisions on service strategy and policy. This meeting organization, formed in 1997, establishes and operates customer satisfaction management policies, plans company human resources related to customer services, operates organizations, and establishes, evaluates, and makes decisions on measures to prevent customer complaints, acting as a foundation for company service enhancement activities and sharing of general customer satisfaction management.

In particular, in relation to quick decision-making on service quality policies and adjusting opinions between departments related to customer service provision standards and procedure, this meeting acts as a core body in which the executives are allowed to make direct decisions for quick, efficient service quality management.

MOTIVATING EMPLOYEES

In addition to customer satisfaction, an airline management team is required to focus on the workforce's satisfaction level. The service quality management requires airlines to evaluate the satisfaction of their workforce as interactions between airline staff and customers directly impact customer satisfaction level.

When an airline creates an enjoyable working environment and shows care and concern for its employees, happy employees have a tendency to perform better at their jobs. This indirectly results in satisfied customers. A research conducted by Watson Watt-a global consulting firm-has shown that when employees are highly engaged, their companies enjoy a 26% increase in employee productivity, have lower turnover risk and are more likely to attract top talent. These companies have also increased overall profit of 1%in the last five years.[11] These employees enjoy going to work and have a positive impact on the company's performance. They are more likely to offer genuine and sincere services and this translates to a higher percentage of return customers. Moreover, customers are likely to spend more money on amenities such as pay upgrade or onboard duty free purchases. According to a research conducted by independent marketing analytics, Ebiquity for American Express in 2014, 74% of surveyed consumers spent more money when they experienced positive customer service from a company.[12]

Happy Employees = Happy Customers

Understanding employees

Many airlines conduct internal surveys and focus groups to better understand their employees, and data pertaining to employee satisfaction can be obtained through satisfaction surveys and focus groups. This allows an airline's management team to recognize the needs of its employees in order to implement appropriate follow-up plans and actions.

Ways to motivate the employees include the following:

Pleasant work environment

Create a friendly work environment that encourages employees to go to work.

Attractive pay

Offer attractive salary

Fairness and transparency

Employees expect to be treated fairly. Being transparent builds trust between a company and its employees.

Empowerment

Allowing employees some autonomy and element level of flexibility in resolving customers' problem can help increase motivation in the workplace.

Extra incentives

Some airlines offer sales commissions as rewards. These include sales related to upselling, upgrading of cabins, excess baggage charges, in-flight food sales and in-flight duty-free sales. This also helps to bring in increase an airline's profit as the employee will take more initiative in selling these extra services to customers.

Offer service in return

Airlines should treat employees in the same way that employees treat customers. This will encourage service agents to work harder as the company will reward them in return. The better an employee serves a customer, the better the company will serve them.

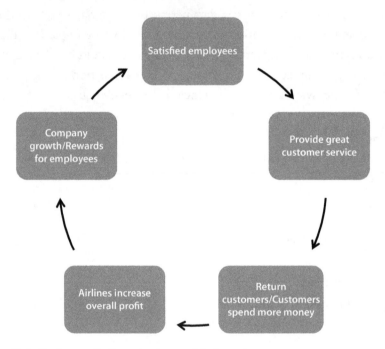

Figure 11-1: Employee motivation and customer satisfaction cycle.

SUMMARY

Airlines need to invest in service quality management so as to continuously improve the quality of its products and services. Airlines may choose from a number of ways to evaluate customer satisfaction level. These include conducting surveys, implementing mystery shopper programs, organizing focus groups and follow-ups on feedback and reviews posted on social media. The data collected is then used to help airlines improve their existing services as well as to create innovative products and services that match customers' expectation. It is equally important that airline provide a good work environment as happy employees create joyful customers.

APPLYING THE KNOWLEDGE

Answer the following questions in complete sentences.

1. Why is service quality management important to an airline?
2. What are mystery shoppers? What do they do?
3. What is a focus group? How can it help an airline to improve its services?
4. Why is it important for an airline to have motivated employees?

ENDNOTES

1. Anonymous. Call center Industry Standard. Call center tips: http://www.callcenterstips.com/CallCenters/CallCenterIndustryStandards.php

2. Hate waiting on hold? Then don't! Fast customer: http://www.fastcustomer.com/

3. Lutz, A. (2012 May 2). REVEALED: How Long Customers Will Stay On Hold Before They Blow Up. Business insider: http://www.businessinsider.com/how-long-customers-will-stay-on-hold-2012-5#ixzz3dwHycbb4

4. Masiter, D. (1985). The Psychology of Waiting Lines.David Maister: http://davidmaister.com/articles/the-psychology-of-waiting-lines/

5. Myant, P. & Abraham, R. (2008). Research on the air passenger experience at Heathrow, Gatwick, Stansted and Manchester airports. ORC International: https://www.caa.co.uk/docs/33/ORC_CAA_report.pdf

6. SITA (2015), 2015 Air Transport industry insight—The baggage report. SITA

7. Kollau, R. (2013 Oct). Air France KLM 'employs' frequent flyers as mystery shoppers, Airlinetrends: http://www.airlinetrends.com/2013/10/15/air-france-klm-employs-frequent-flyers-as-mystery-shoppers/

8. Rydholm, J. (1996, May). In-flight satisfaction research keeps United Airlines customer oriented. Quirk's: http://www.quirks.com/articles/a1996/19960505.aspx

9. Bachelor, L. (2012, May 12). Complain on Twitter for an instant response, the guardian, Guardian News and Media Limited.

10. Asiana Airlines. (2015). Customer Satisfaction Management. Asiana Airlines: https://kr.flyasiana.com/C/en/homepage.do?menuId=005006002001000&menuType=CMS

11. Watson, W. (2010). Watson Wyatt's WorkUSA Survey Identifies Steps to Keep Employees Engaged & Productive: http://knowledgepay.com/workusa0809/

12. Clack, J. 2014. (2014) American Express Global Customer Service Barometer, Ebiduity: http://about.americanexpress.com/news/docs/2014x/2014-Global-Customer-Service-Barometer-US.pdf

CHAPTER TWELVE

Selling Techniques and Contemporary Customer Service

Chapter Outline

Learning Objectives

After reading this chapter, the reader should be able to:

- Understand the difference between upsell and cross-sell
- Recognize customers' buying decision process
- Identify the selling process
- Understand the shift in contemporary customer service

CONTEMPORARY CUSTOMER SERVICE
AND SELLING TECHNIQUES

All service agents are encouraged to promote an airline's products as offering what customers need helps to increase customer satisfaction and leads to better customer service performance.

Upsell and cross-sell

Many airlines now offer upselling programs and service agents are responsible for promoting these additional services. Upselling is a strategy that encourages customers to purchase a comparable higher-end product than the one in question at a premium cost. These products may differ in quality, starting from a base model and progressing through more luxurious models with additional features.[1] Airlines usually offer a mix of tangible and intangible products (refer to Chapter 1) that are available for upselling.

However, some airlines only offer upsell products to frequent flyers and loyal customers. Below are a few examples:

- A customer books an economy class trip to London for $840 and is given the opportunity to upgrade to business-class cabin for an additional $150. Some airlines reserve upsell products to selected customer as an incentive for their loyalty to the airline.
- A customer who has purchased a discounted ticket pays for an upsell in order to enjoy more flexibility and avoid flight restrictions.
- A customer assigned to a middle seat pays a nominal fee to get a seat by the exit row for more leg space.

The best way to recommend an upsell to customers is to make a comparison between what they have already purchased with the upgraded product.

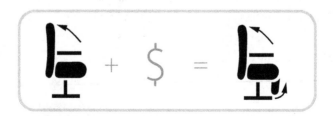

Figure 12-1: Upsell—paying extra for more comfort.

Cross-selling, on the other hand, identifies products that satisfy additional, complementary needs that are unfulfilled by the original item that has already been purchased.[2] Often times, cross-selling points users to products they would have purchased anyway; and by presenting them at the right time, service agents can make a successful sale. Cross-selling usually takes place during the customer reservation process and within the aircraft cabin. As such, service agents need to pay attention to the additional items customers are may be interested in. Below are some examples of cross-selling:

- Customers purchase their air tickets, and book their hotel accommodation and car rental via the airlines' website.
- A customer purchases a digital camera during a flight and the cabin crew asks the customer if he/she would like to buy a memory card.
- A customer orders a plate of chicken rice while on-board a low-cost carrier and a cabin crew staff asks the customer if he/she would like to buy a beverage or dessert.
- A customer traveling on economy class purchases a one-time business lounge access to access the lounge facilities.
- Customers purchasing priority boarding service so as to board the aircraft before other passengers.

Figure 12-2: Example, Cross-sell.

Upselling usually takes place at the check-in counter as customers finalize their flight arrangements. These days, some airlines also offer upselling in the cabin and cabin crew need to use a credit card scanner. This allows customers visibility to inspect what they are getting before the purchase, such as in the instance of a cabin class upgrade in which customers can have a look at the additional amenities provided.[3]

Upselling and cross-selling offer opportunities for customers to choose from a variety of better and up-scale products. As such, some airlines even consider it a failure to not recommend a better offer to customers when such options are available.

Service agents with the ability to upsell often help to increase customer satisfaction as well as improve an airline's profits. Products and services available for upsell include seats, lounge access, in-flight services, in-flight amenities and duty-free sales.

Service agents must also be honest and provide accurate information when promoting these products and services, and refrain from provided any unrelated information that may potentially damage the trust they have already developed with customers.

Figure 12-3: Various airline products available for upselling.

Selling skill refers to the ability to influence customers' decision to purchase. As majority of customers have already bought their air tickets before arriving at the airport, there is little chance for service agents to demonstrate their selling skills. However, many airlines continue to include sales channels both at the airport and on-board a flight as they give customers the opportunity to purchase upgrades or additional products. This is extremely important for low-cost airlines whereby customers have the option of purchasing add-on services.

The buyer decision process

The buyer decision process represents a number of stages that a customer will go through before actually making the final purchase decision. According to Philip Kotler, a renowned American marketing author and consultant, this consists of the following 6 stages: need recognition, information search, evaluation of alternatives, purchase decision and post-purchase behavior.[4]

Need recognition

The buying decision starts with a customer's recognition of a need that is made aware of by word of mouth or advertisements. These needs can only be addressed when a product or service is available.

Information search

After recognizing the need, the customer will seek to get more information about a product or service that fulfills the needs. The customer will then inquire more about the product or service.

Evaluation of alternatives

The customer makes a logical and careful calculation to evaluate whether a particular purchase is worthwhile. They will also evaluate other alternative product or services that can fulfill the same needs.

Purchase decision

The customer will make a decision as to whether to make the purchase of a particular product or service after evaluating its values.

Post-purchase behavior

Post-purchase behavior determines whether a customer is satisfied or dissatisfied with the purchased product or services.

Buyer decision Process	At the airport	In-flight		
Need recognition	More comfort	More comfort	Hunger	Purchase a gift
Information search	Seat upgrade	Seat upgrade	What food is available for sale	What products are available
Evaluation of alternatives	Empty seat next to assigned seat	Empty seat next to assigned seat	Choice of food available	What brands are available
Purchase decision	Purchase extra seat or upgrade	Purchase extra seat or upgrade	Purchase selected in-flight meal	Purchase in-flight product
Post-purchase behavior	Is the seat upgrade worth the cost, i.e. Will this make my flight experience more comfortable?	Is the seat upgrade worth the cost i.e. Will this make my flight experience more comfortable?	Is the food delicious?	Is the gift value for money?

| Need recognition | Information search | Evaluation of alternatives | Purchase decision | Post-purchase behavior |

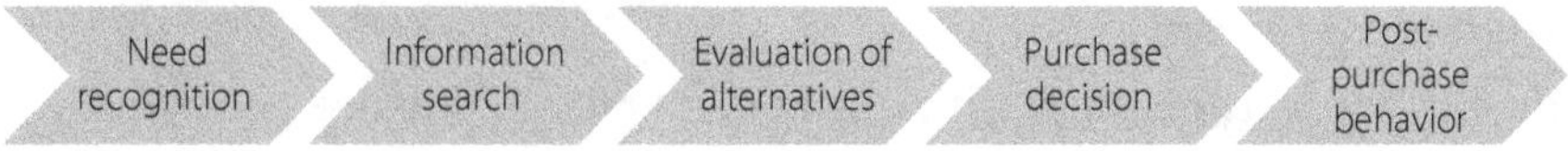

Figure 12-4: The buyer decision process.

ESSENTIAL SELLING SKILLS

Product knowledge

To be successful in upselling, service agents must have in-depth knowledge of an airline's products. They must also understand how these products or services can add value and comfort to customers and be able to explain the benefits to the customers.

Ability to read customers' mind

Not all customers are willing to purchase additional products. As such, service agents must have the ability to identify potential customers and their needs before approaching them for upselling or cross-selling. For example, it is less likely for a family of four customers to make a purchase of a cabin upgrade as compared to a solo traveler.

Product pitching

After identifying a potential customer for upselling, service agents can suggest suitable products and services for upselling and cross-selling, and pique these potential customers' interests by informing them about these offers. Service agents can also choose to market these products and services as exclusive promotions that are only available to loyal or elite customers.

Service agent: Mr. James, I am pleased to inform you there is an exclusive offer on today's flight, and you are eligible to purchase an upgrade at a special price. This offer is only extended to frequent flyers.

Product explanation

Service agents need to explain the features and highlight the benefits of the different products. They can also show potential customers images of the products if necessary.

The selling process

Successful salespeople take the time to hone their skills and are constantly iterating to better help their prospects. Below is a breakdown of the popular 5-stage selling model, comprising of relationship, interest, persuasion, want and closing.

Relationship

A sale can only take place when a relationship has been established between service agents and customers. Customers generally prefer to speak with friendly staff members, hence greeting customers with respect and demonstrating helpfulness will help to develop trust and build relationship.

Interest

Once a relationship is established, service agents may then find out more about customers' interest in the various products and services that are available for upselling or cross-selling.

Persuasion

If customers show signs of interest, service agents can then explain the functions, values and benefits of these products and services.

Service agent: With the cabin upgrade, you'll be able to take a good rest in the comfortable business-class seat before your important meeting in Singapore tomorrow morning.

Patience

Allow time for customers to consider a purchase. Do not close the sale before the customer makes a decision as this will come across as being too pushy.

Close the sale

If customers cannot make a decision as to whether to make a purchase, it is the service agent's responsibility to ask them about their considerations. There may be instances whereby service agents can actually help customers to make a decision that is in their best interest.

Figure 12-5: The five-step selling process.

Dos and Don'ts

Dos

Be prepared

- Service agents should prepare a basic script ahead of time to inform customers about the products and services that are available for upselling or cross-selling.
- Service agents should have adequate knowledge of these products and services.

Chose the right timing

- Choose the right timing to promote products and services, i.e. do not suggest upselling or cross-selling to customers who are in a rush to catch their flights
- Only offer upselling of seats to customers who have requested for these

Demonstrate benefits

- Demonstrate how customers can benefit from the purchase
- Explain that the purchased product or service is the solution to their problem

Service agent: The cabin upgrade entitles you to a more comfortable seat which can be turned into a flat bed. You will also get a personal entertainment system and free Wi-Fi service during the flight. This offer is only available to our selected customers.

Maintain service standards
- Continue to offer existing service to customers even if they decline to make an additional purchase
- Maintain friendly attitude and service even when customers decline to make an additional purchase

Don'ts
Give pressure
- Don't pressure customers to make additional purchases
- Allow time for customers to make a decision instead of imposing your views on them

Repeat the message
- Service teams should offer upselling and cross-selling of products and services at one single location so that customers are not approached by multiple service staff promoting the same offers

Ask close-ended questions
Avoiding asking close-ended when promoting products and services as customers have a higher tendency to decline such attempts to upsell or cross-sell. Instead, keep a lookout for opportunities to upsell or cross-sell, and steer conversations towards such offers.

Do	Don't
We are offering a special promotion on today's flight for seat upgrades. This will allow you to have more space for stretching your legs.	Would you like to purchase an upsell?

Get upset

- It is normal for customers not to make an additional purchase. Service agents should not be upset when customers decline such offers.

Do	Don't
Be prepared	Give pressure
Choose the right timing	Repeat the message
Demonstrate the benefits	Asking close–ended questions
Maintain service standards	Get upset

CONTEMPORARY CUSTOMER SERVICE

The use of mobile phones has become very common these days and many customers now expect airlines to be contactable around the clock. As such, having a 24-hour call center allows customers to receive support assistance at any time, especially for airlines that operate international routes. It also allows airlines to divert calls from different countries to one central call center, hence offering convenience to customers across the globe.

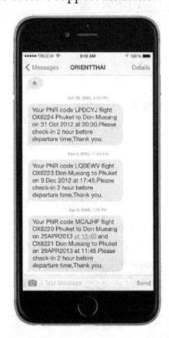

Text messages

Many customers now prefer to communicate with service agents via text messages. As such, an increasing number of airlines are using text messages as a means of interacting with customers. This is another form of 24-hour service that offers convenience to customers.

Live chat

Live chat is another communication channel that has become increasingly important. Customers can easily communicate directly with service agents via an airline's live chat

Figure 12-6: An airline using technology to connect with passengers.

function embedded in the company's website. This is a much more convenient means of communication and customers can work on other tasks whilst chatting with service agents.

Many airlines are also using customer virtual assistant systems that have been pre-programmed to answer frequently asked questions. The systems are linked to databases that automatically generate answers based on certain keywords.

Social media

Social media is a vital means of communication that provides essential company information and promotions to customers. The chat function embedded within most social media platform also functions as a real-time chat room that allows an airline and its customers to interact. This is increasingly important in today's consumer market as opinions expressed on social media can have a huge impact on an airline's brand and reputation.

Figure 12-7: Airline's virtual chat functions. *Reprinted with permission from Jetstar.*

Self service

Airlines are also offering automated systems that allow customers to make purchases through the Internet or phone, check-in for their flight and board the aircraft without interacting with service agents. These self-services systems provide more flexibility in terms of carrying out simple standard transactions and processes such as purchasing of air tickets online and retrieving of boarding passes via the self-service check-in kiosk.

Multichannel customer contact

Customers no longer contact airlines through a single means and tech-savvy customers usually make use of the most convenient channels available. Cloud technologies allow different channels to be linked up so that airlines can track customers' flight record and purchasing habits easily. Cloud technology also makes it easier for airlines to interact with their customers anywhere and at any time. These technologies are useful in helping airlines to forge a closer relationship with customers.

THE SHIFT IN CUSTOMER CARE

Airlines are increasingly replacing traditional service agents' functions with technology to reduce operating cost. Today, customers might not even have any interaction with service agents until they board the aircraft.

However, these technologies can be easily adopted by other competitors and at the end of the day, customer service agents are the ones who can make a difference. Customers seek personalized services; they wanted to be respected, taken care of and they want the intimate interactions that technology cannot offer.

Technology can help to speed up processes but machines are not capable of solving all customers' problem. Furthermore, technology can fail, such as in the instance of power outages and computer system failure. In such situations, service agents will need to issue hand-written boarding passes.

Hence customer care continues to play an important role in the airline service industry. For example, all systems operated using technology will be down during a power outage and service agents are still required to reboots the system.

Figure 12-8: During computer outage, service agents will need to issue hand-written boarding passes. *(Photo courtesy of Miha Rekar).*

Maintaining lifelong customers

The most successful businesses have retained long-term and lifelong loyal customers. This group of customers allows airlines to maintain a stable source of income.

SUMMARY

Selling of products and services is part of all airline service agents' job and responsibility. As such, it is vital for service agents to have an in-depth understanding of customers' buying decision process in order for them to offer appropriate products and services.

While there is an increasing trend of technology replacing service agents in the area of customer service, the latter can never be fully replaced as soft skills cannot be replaced by technology, and customers seek personalized services.

APPLYING THE KNOWLEDGE

Answer the following questions in complete sentences.

1. What are the differences between upselling and cross-selling?
2. Explain a customer's buying decision process with regards to purchasing a seat upgrade.
3. Refer to the 5-stage selling process and explain how each step is used to sell a bottle of perfume on-board a flight.
4. List and explain the different types of contemporary customer service.

ENDNOTES

1. Lewis, J. Differences Between Up-Selling and Cross Selling. Chron: http://smallbusiness.chron.com/differences-between-upselling-cross-selling-30519.html

2. Schwartz, K. (2013, May 16). Cross-selling is defined as selling an additional product when the customer is purchasing the original product. Customer Service Investigator: http://csi.softwareadvice.com/3-best-practices-for-upselling-and-cross-selling-in-customer-service-interactions-0419/

3. Leocha, C. (2009, Apr 20). Upsell Tactics-Legitimate or Bait and Switch? Consumer traveler: http://consumertraveler.com/today/upsell-tactics-%E2%80%94-legitimate-or-bait-and-switch/

4. Kotler, P. & Armstrong, G. (2010). Principle of Marketing. Pearson.

Index